LIFE
ALBUM
A YEAR IN
PICTURES

1997

1997
A YEAR IN PICTURES

EDITOR Killian Jordan
PICTURE EDITOR Barbara Baker Burrows
ART DIRECTOR Sharon Okamoto
DEPUTY PICTURE EDITOR Dot McMahon
ASSOCIATE PICTURE EDITOR Maggie Berkvist
PHOTO RESEARCH Neal Jackson
WRITERS Romy Pokorny, Pamela Stock, Emily Listfield
DESIGN ASSISTANT Melanie deForest
ART INTERN Victor Williams
COPY EDITOR Melissa Wohlgemuth
PAGE CODER Albert Rufino
And all members of the LIFE Copy Department

Time Inc. Home Entertainment
MANAGING DIRECTOR David Gitow
DIRECTOR, CONTINUITIES AND SINGLE SALES David Arfine
DIRECTOR, CONTINUITIES AND RETENTION Michael Barrett
DIRECTOR, NEW PRODUCTS Alicia Longobardo
GROUP PRODUCT MANAGERS Robert Fox, Michael Holahan
PRODUCT MANAGERS Christopher Berzolla, Stacy Hirschberg,
Amy Jacobsson, Jennifer McLyman, Dan Melore
MANAGER, RETAIL AND NEW MARKETS Thomas Mifsud
ASSOCIATE PRODUCT MANAGERS Louisa Bartle, Alison Ehrmann,
Carlos Jimenez, Nancy London, Dawn Perry, Daria Raehse
ASSISTANT PRODUCT MANAGERS Meredith Shelley, Betty Su
EDITORIAL OPERATIONS DIRECTOR John Calvano
FULFILLMENT DIRECTOR Michelle Gudema
FINANCIAL DIRECTOR Tricia Griffin
ASSOCIATE FINANCIAL MANAGER Amy Maselli
MARKETING ASSISTANT Sarah Holmes

Consumer Marketing Division
PRODUCTION DIRECTOR John E. Tighe
BOOK PRODUCTION MANAGER Jessica McGrath
BOOK PRODUCTION COORDINATOR Joseph Napolitano

SPECIAL THANKS TO Donna Miano-Ferrara, Anna Yelenskaya

PICTURE SOURCES are listed by page. Cover: Kim Knott/Camera Press/Retna; insets from left, The Kobal Collection; Remi Benali-Stephen Ferry/Gamma Liaison; Ho/Reuters/Archive Photos; Raghu Rai/Magnum Photos. Back cover: from top left, Alberto Pizzoli/Sygma; Stephen Crowley/New York Times Pictures; Eric Hylden/Grand Forks Herald; Steven Freeman; Peter Byrne; Les Stone/Sygma. 24, 60, 98 and 130: styling by Ellen Glasston. 24: Mehndi painting by Nayna Patel. 26: Tamagotchi: Xavier Rossi/Gamma Liaison. 27: C. Love: Michael Caulfield/AP/Wide World Photos; C. Gooding Jr.: Reed Saxon/AP/Wide World Photos. 44-45: Wide World Photos. 62: Becky: Rachel Montana/Corbis. 63: M. Jordan: Scott Cunningham/NBA Photos. 64: H. Doody: Archive Photos; B. Crystal: J. Varriale/Outline; GOODNIGHT MOON: © 1947 by Harper & Row, text © renewed 1975 by Roberta Brown Rauch, illustrations © by Clement Hurd renewed 1975; Ajax: Peter Weidlein. 65: Matisse's JAZZ: Giraudon/Art Resource, NY. 96-97: Wide World Photos. 102: From THE CAT IN THE HAT by Dr. Seuss™ and © 1957 and renewed 1985 by Dr. Seuss Enterprises, L.P. by permission of Random House. 135: Recorder: Ewing Galloway.

Copyright 1998
Time Inc. Home Entertainment

Published by

Books
Time Inc.
1271 Avenue of the Americas
New York, New York 10020

First Edition
ISBN 1-883013-29-1 ISSN 1092-0463
"LIFE" is a registered trademark of Time Inc.

PRINTED IN THE UNITED STATES OF AMERICA

FOUNDER Henry R. Luce 1898-1967

EDITOR-IN-CHIEF Norman Pearlstine
EDITORIAL DIRECTOR Henry Muller
EDITOR OF NEW MEDIA Daniel Okrent

CHAIRMAN, CEO Don Logan
EXECUTIVE VICE PRESIDENTS Elizabeth Valk Long, Jim Nelson, Joseph A. Ripp

MANAGING EDITOR Isolde Motley
DEPUTY MANAGING EDITOR Susan Bolotin
ASSISTANT MANAGING EDITOR David Friend (Director of Photography)
DIRECTOR OF DESIGN Tom Bentkowski
SENIOR EDITORS Robert Friedman, Killian Jordan, Melissa Stanton, Robert Sullivan
CHIEF OF REPORTERS June Omura Goldberg
COPY CHIEF Robert Andreas
PICTURE EDITOR Marie Schumann
PICTURE EDITOR FOR SPECIAL PROJECTS Barbara Baker Burrows
DEPUTY ART DIRECTOR Sharon Okamoto
WRITERS Allison Adato, Vanessa Bush, George Howe Colt, Claudia Glenn Dowling, Charles Hirshberg, Marilyn Johnson, Kenneth Miller
ASSOCIATE EDITORS Anne Hollister, Sasha Nyary, Joshua R. Simon
SENIOR REPORTER Jen M.R. Doman
REPORTERS Harriet Barovick, Jimmie Briggs, Cynthia Fox
RESEARCH ASSISTANTS Priya Giri, Rakisha Kearns-White
STAFF PHOTOGRAPHER Joe McNally
ASSOCIATE PICTURE EDITOR Dubravka Bondulic
ASSISTANT PICTURE EDITORS Azurea Lee Dudley, Vivette Porges
PICTURE DESK Suzette-Ivonne Rodriguez (Department Coordinator), Chris Whelan (Traffic Coordinator), Hélène Veret (Paris), Edward Nana Osei-Bonsu (Financial Manager)
ASSISTANT ART DIRECTOR Sam Serebin
ART ASSISTANT Melanie deForest
TECHNOLOGY MANAGER Michael T. Rose
DEPUTY TECHNOLOGY MANAGER Steve Walkowiak
COPY DESK Madeleine Edmondson (Deputy), Nikki Amdur, Christine McNulty, Larry Nesbitt, Albert Rufino
FINANCIAL MANAGER Eileen M. Kelly
ADMINISTRATION Barbara Fox
CONTRIBUTING EDITORS Lisa Grunwald, Richard B. Stolley
SPECIAL CORRESPONDENTS Jenny Allen, Todd Brewster (New York), Judy Ellis (Los Angeles), Linda Gomez (Sacramento), Sue Allison (Washington), Mimi Murphy (Rome), Tala Skari (Paris)
CONTRIBUTING PHOTOGRAPHERS Harry Benson (Contract), David Burnett, Enrico Ferorelli, Donna Ferrato, Dana Fineman, Frank Fournier, Henry Groskinsky, Gregory Heisler, Derek Hudson, Lynn Johnson, Brian Lanker, Andy Levin, John Loengard, Mary Ellen Mark, Michael Melford, Carl Mydans, James Nachtwey, Lennart Nilsson, Michael O'Neill, Gordon Parks, Co Rentmeester, Eugene Richards, Bob Sacha, David Turnley
LIFE PICTURE SALES Maryann Kornely (Director)

PUBLISHER Edward R. McCarrick
ASSOCIATE PUBLISHER/ADVERTISING Donald B. Fries
ADVERTISING SALES New York: Peter S. Krieger (Eastern Advertising Director), Kristen Fairback, Michael Hollis, Patrick J. O'Donnell, George Walter, Michael Wolfe
Chicago: Ney V. Raahauge (Midwest Advertising Director), Stephen D. Krupkin
Detroit: P. Thornton Withers (Detroit Advertising Director), Tracey K. Pierce
Los Angeles: Janet Haire (Western Advertising Director), Lynnette Ward
San Francisco: William G. Smith (Manager)
Special Representatives: Dean Zeko (Dallas), Peter Carr (San Diego and Mexico)
MARKETING/FRANCHISE DEVELOPMENT Mark L. Hintsa (Director), Gianine DeSimone (Manager)
SALES DEVELOPMENT Claudia L. Jepsen (Director), Michelle Olofson, Allison M. Ziering (Managers), Jennifer Reed (Art Director), Marybeth Burnell (Design Associate)
CONSUMER MARKETING Monika Winn (Director), Anita Raisch (Planning Manager), Marilou M. Owens (Renewals Manager), Samuel Tisdale (Assistant Manager), Cindy Cohen (Marketing Assistant)
BUSINESS OFFICE Nancy J. Phillips (Financial Director), Nancy Blank, Mario Guerrero, Dawn Vezirian (Managers)
PRODUCTION Murray Goldwaser (Director), Steven Bessenoff, Jill Gerlin, Len Lieberman (Managers), Yvonne Parker (Assistant Manager)
PUBLIC RELATIONS Alison Hart Cirenza (Director), Marina M. Hoffmann (Assistant)
ADMINISTRATION Adrienne Hegarty, Meghan Anderson, Theresa Coffey, Lisa DiPressi, Nancy J. Harrar, Caroline Hoover, Kristin Palizzi, Amy Ryan, Ann Spohrer

TIME INC.
SENIOR EXECUTIVE EDITOR Frank Lalli
EXECUTIVE EDITORS Joëlle Attinger, José M. Ferrer III
DEVELOPMENT EDITOR Jacob Young
EDITORIAL SERVICES Sheldon Czapnik (Director), Claude Boral (General Manager), Thomas E. Hubbard (Photo Lab), Lany Walden McDonald (Research Center), Beth Bencini Zarcone (Picture Collection), Thomas Smith (Technology), James Macove (Marketing), Maryann Kornely (Syndication)
EDITORIAL TECHNOLOGY Paul Zazzera (Vice President), Damien Creavin (Director)

LIFE

ALBUM

A YEAR IN
PICTURES

CONTENTS

Princess Diana's funeral
procession, London,
September 6, 1997

JANUARY FEBRUARY MARCH

Seeing Double

Science gone mad or face of the future? While Dolly, the first cloned mammal, looks great, ethicists wonder if she's not one sheep too many. Created by a little-known British embryologist from a single cell, Dolly is in essence her mother's identical twin. We're looking forward to seeing them explain *that* on *Oprah*.

JAN. 1 New! Voluntary! TV's ratings system, based on the one used by the Motion Picture Association of America, goes into effect. Categories range from TV-Y **(suitable for all audiences)** to TV-M (not for viewers under 17).

JAN. 3 After 15 years, Bryant Gumbel ends his tenure as cohost of NBC's *Today*. **His send-off** includes a poem by colleague Katie Couric and surprise guests like Muhammad Ali. Replaced by news anchor Matt Lauer, Gumbel will later accept a $1-million-per-year deal with CBS for his own weekly prime-time show.

JAN. 7 Newt Gingrich is reelected **speaker of the House,** despite accusations of improperly accepting tax-free donations and misleading investigators about his actions. He will become the first speaker in 208 years to be formally reprimanded and fined.

JAN. 12 Citing harassment and abuse by upperclassmen, two of the four female cadets at The Citadel announce **they are dropping out.** Police confirm that the women had not only been forced to sing sexually explicit songs, they were also doused with nail polish remover and their clothing set on fire.

Having a Ball

It was her dad's big night, but for Chelsea, looking very va-va-voom backstage at an Inaugural Ball, it was her time to shine. The Clintons did an admirable job of keeping her under wraps—for a while. But now all is revealed: They love the First Daughter just the way non-heads-of-state love their own kids. To the max.

JAN. 15 Weight Watchers International names **Sarah Ferguson, Duchess of York,** as its celebrity spokesperson. Her reported salary for promoting the weight-loss plan: more than $1 million. One ad, which uses the word "paparazzi," will be pulled after the death of Princess Diana.

JAN. 16 Ennis Cosby, 27, the real-life son of **beloved TV dad Bill Cosby,** is shot to death on a Los Angeles freeway. The suspected motive of the man charged with the murder is robbery. Of Ennis, the elder Cosby says, "He was my hero."

JAN. 16 Two bombs explode at an abortion clinic in Atlanta, injuring seven people. The incident coincides with **the 24th anniversary** of *Roe* v. *Wade.*

JAN. 17 Basketball's Dennis Rodman is suspended for 11 games for **kicking a cameraman.** The Chicago Bulls' star rebounder is also fined $25,000 and ordered to seek psychological help. Next? A $50,000 fine for an insulting remark about Mormons.

Drive-by Chuting

Not everyone takes to the front porch during retirement. Former President George Bush, 72, jumped out of an airplane 12,500 feet over Yuma, Ariz., reenacting a jump he was forced to make in 1944 when ground fire hit the torpedo bomber he was flying. He recalls the earlier leap as "pure terror." This time it looks like pure pleasure.

11

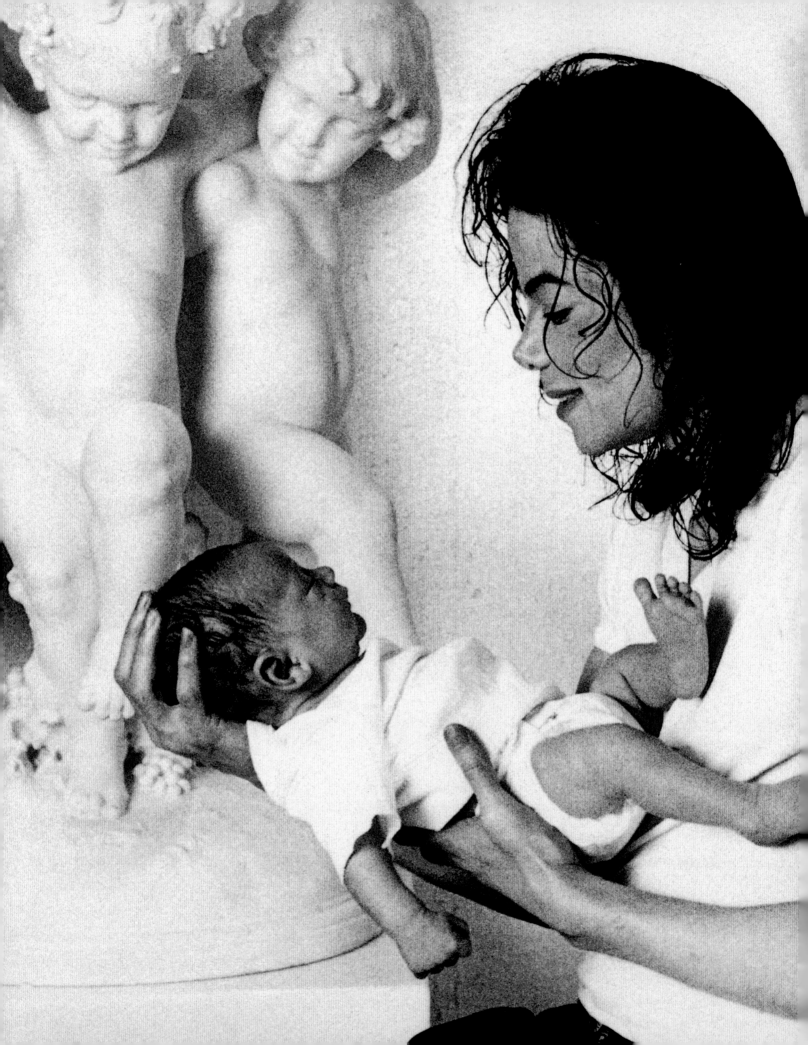

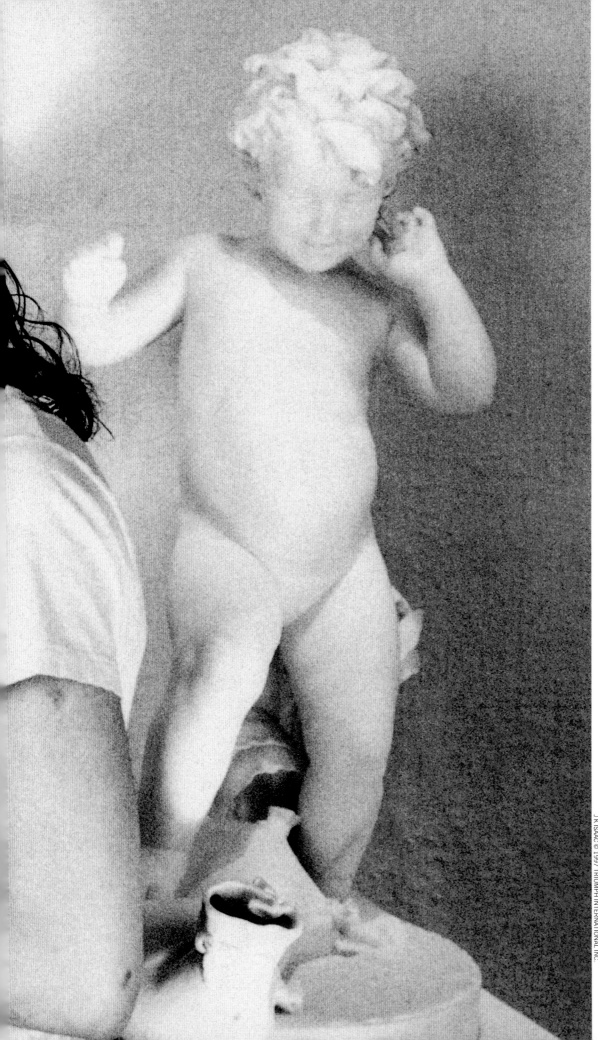

JAN. 26 The Green Bay Packers' 35-21 win over the New England Patriots in Super Bowl XXXI is the team's **first NFL title** since their back-to-back victories in 1967 and 1968.

JAN. 29 Bowing to pressure from angry customers and three dozen state attorneys general, **America Online** agrees to hand out refunds to users of its overburdened network. Many of AOL's eight million members had been getting busy signals instead of getting online. An E-mail from AOL chairman Steve Case, asking subscribers to "try to show some restraint" during peak evening hours, was greeted with 17,000 angry replies—crashing his computer's mailbox.

JAN. 30-31 Videotapes from 1991 and 1993, depicting a brutal hazing exercise at Camp Lejeune in North Carolina, air on national television: Marine Corps paratroopers are seen having newly earned jump pins pounded into their chests, **a ritual known as blood pinning.** Secretary of Defense William S. Cohen says he is "disturbed and disgusted" by what he sees on the tapes and will strictly enforce a "zero-tolerance" antihazing policy.

Heir Apparent

It's not exactly a Norman Rockwell image of fatherhood, but . . . this family man gets to do things his own way. After the birth of his son, Prince, Michael Jackson said he didn't want him to grow up in a "fishbowl." A month later he sold family photos to a British magazine for a reported $2 million. We'll forgive the inconsistency, though—the proceeds were earmarked for charity.

13

JAN. 31 The 1977 blockbuster *Star Wars* returns to movie theaters nationwide. *The Empire Strikes Back* and *Return of the Jedi*—the second and third installments of the sci-fi trilogy—will also be rereleased. Three *Star Wars* **prequels are in the works;** they will reveal the origins of Darth Vader and Obi-Wan Kenobi.

FEB. 4 A civil jury in Santa Monica, Calif., **finds O.J. Simpson liable** in the deaths of his ex-wife Nicole and Ronald Goldman (although Simpson was acquitted in a criminal court trial) and orders Simpson to pay $33.5 million in compensatory and punitive damages. Television's legal saga of the century may finally be over, but the networks face a near crisis when cameras barely manage to cut to the announcement of the verdict as President Clinton's State of the Union Address concludes.

FEB. 4 The Army's **top enlisted man,** Sgt. Maj. Gene C. McKinney, is accused of sexually assaulting his female assistant. Five more female soldiers will come forward with charges against him. McKinney is suspended for poor job performance; later he will be stripped of his title. He pleads not guilty at his arraignment.

A Nation Bilked

In March, when the Albanian government's failed pyramid schemes caused well over half of the country's households to lose their savings, citizens took to the streets in protest. Eventually, 7,000 European troops were called in to contain the violence. Order slowly returned, but Prime Minister Fatos Nano, who took over in July, admits that "to rebuild this country will take a long time."

FEB. 6 President Clinton presents his **$1.69 trillion budget** for fiscal year 1998 to Congress. The President promises that the plan will balance the budget by 2002.

FEB. 13 A *Washington Post* report says the Justice Department has evidence that **the Chinese government** sought to direct contributions to the Democratic National Committee before President Clinton's reelection. At the same time, key former administration figures refuse, for now, to cooperate with a House inquiry into improper fund-raising.

FEB. 15 Invoking the Railway Labor Act of 1926, President Clinton helps avert a major strike by American Airlines pilots. The carrier's chief executive is pleased, but some **employees are cooler:** "Basically, [Clinton] castrated the union," says one.

FEB. 23 A gunman opens fire on the 86th-floor observation deck of New York City's **Empire State Building,** killing one and wounding six. The shooter—Ali Abu Kamal, a 69-year-old Palestinian—then turns the .380 semiautomatic on himself and dies.

Madame Secretary

Every new job brings a slight change of identity, but for new Secretary of State Madeleine Albright (here, bussing outgoing Secretary Warren Christopher), it went deeper: She learned that her Czechoslovak parents, who had raised her as a Catholic, were Jewish-born; three of her grandparents perished in the Holocaust. Albright handled these revelations as she grappled with an expanding NATO and a fractious Middle East.

FEB. 28 For the first time since 1981, when AIDS was pronounced an epidemic, the Centers for Disease Control and Prevention in Atlanta reports that the number of deaths from the disease has dropped—about 12 percent. **The encouraging statistics** are, according to the agency, thanks to the success of new drug therapies, as well as better access to care and increased financing for treatment.

MAR. 1–2 Tornadoes and floods tear through eight states, splintering homes and killing more than 40 people. The devastating storms cause drownings in Ohio and Tennessee and fatal winds in Texas and Mississippi. **Arkansas is the hardest hit:** 25 are dead; ultimately, 23 counties will be declared disaster areas.

MAR. 3 Vice President Al Gore acknowledges making campaign fund-raising phone calls from the White House. Though he says, **"I am proud of what I did;** I do not feel like I did anything wrong, much less illegal," he vows to refrain from such solicitations in the future.

Hearts on Fire

The year began with Israeli-Palestinian peace negotiations. Within three months, talks had ceased and violence escalated. The hot-button issue: control of the West Bank city of Hebron. As the peace talks faltered, scenes like this one—of a young Palestinian hurling a gasoline bomb at Israeli troops—became all too familiar.

18

RULA HALAWANI/REUTERS/ARCHIVE PHOTOS

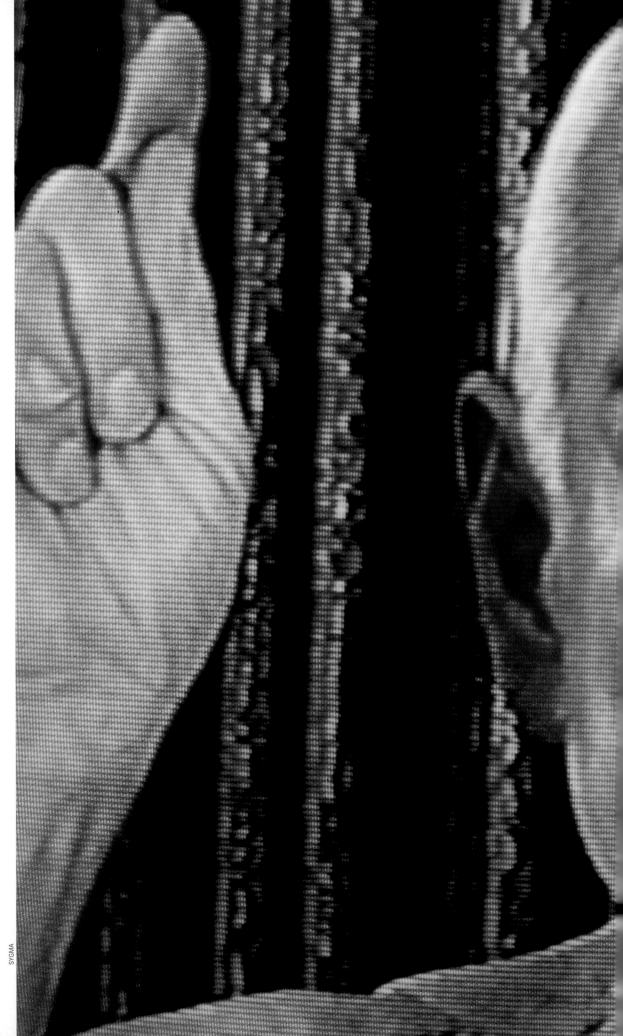

MAR. 9 The NBA debuts a sleek campaign to promote the **Women's National Basketball Association.** Television spots show the women practicing on a court. There are no words except the slogan, "We Got Next."

MAR. 11 The title "Sir" is officially added to Paul McCartney's name. Fellow former Beatles Ringo Starr and George Harrison, according to **Sir Paul,** "call me 'Your Holiness.'"

MAR. 11 Five female Army recruits say that investigators coerced them into **making false accusations** of sexual misconduct against officers at Maryland's Aberdeen Proving Ground. The women say they had been promised immunity from prosecution if they testified and threatened with retaliation if they did not.

MAR. 14 President Clinton takes a tumble—**not in popularity ratings,** but rather on the front steps of golfer Greg Norman's house. The slip tears a tendon in his right kneecap, requiring a two-hour operation to repair.

Followers, Beware

He used videos and the Internet to preach a weird mix of androgyny and intergalactic salvation. Marshall Applewhite told his Heaven's Gate followers their bodies were "containers" to be left behind as they traveled to the "next level." The method of transportation? A spaceship trailing the comet Hale-Bopp. When police found the cult members' bodies in a California mansion, they had five-dollar bills in their pockets and flight bags by their sides.

SYGMA

MAR. 20 The Liggett Group, smallest of the major U.S. cigarette makers, admits that **smoking is addictive and causes cancer** and that tobacco companies have marketed their products to children for decades. The concessions are central to Liggett's settlement of 22 states' lawsuits accusing the industry of hiding the truth about the dangers of tobacco.

MAR. 25 The Federal Reserve votes to **raise interest rates** for the first time in more than two years as a precaution against the well-hidden threat of inflation. By inching up (one quarter of a percent) the federal funds target rate for overnight loans between banks, the central bank hopes to slow economic growth and to constrain significant wage and price increases.

MAR. 27 Dexter King, 36, son of slain civil rights leader Dr. Martin Luther King Jr., meets with James Earl Ray, **his father's convicted killer,** in the Nashville prison where Ray is serving a 99-year sentence for the assassination. The prisoner, 69 years old and suffering from liver cancer, asserts his innocence in the 1968 shooting—to which King surprisingly responds, "I believe you, and my family believes you."

Light from Above

The 25-mile-wide Hale-Bopp comet spread earthly commotion as it streaked across the sky this spring. To astronomers it revealed astonishing clues about how the earth was formed. To average stargazers, Hale-Bopp's visibility was astounding. "You could call this a people's comet," said J. Kelly Beatty of *Sky and Telescope* magazine. Except, perhaps, for those 39 people in the Heaven's Gate cult to whom this thing of beauty was an invitation to suicide.

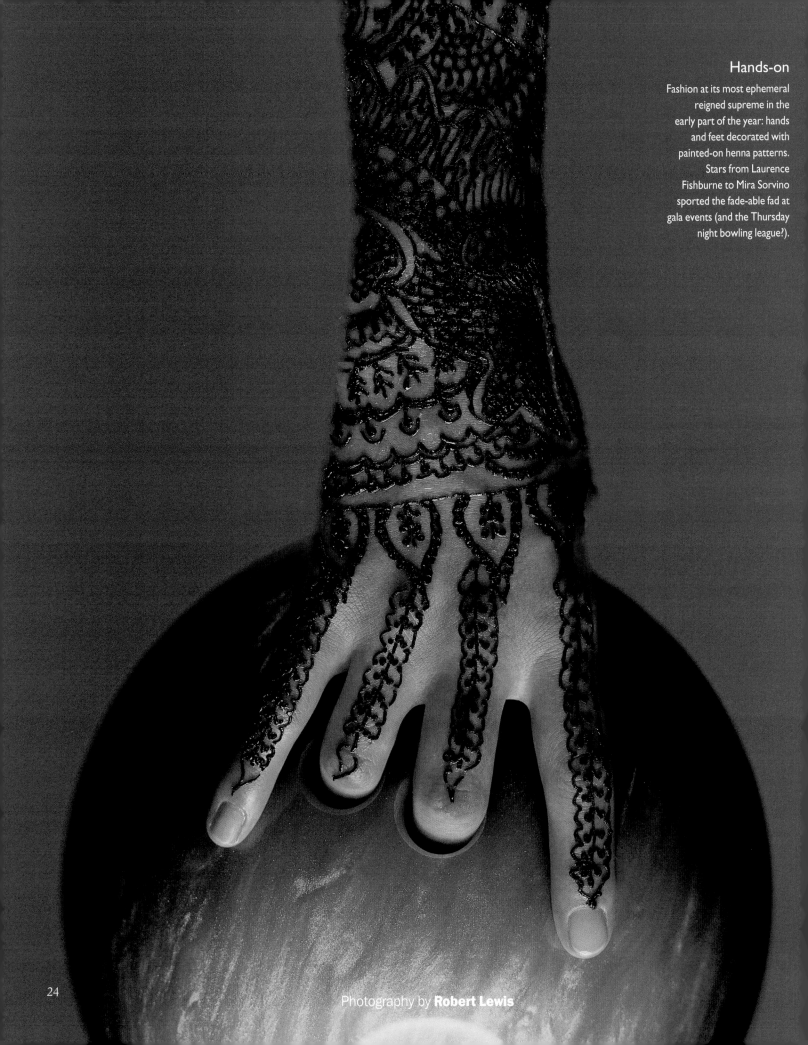

Fashion at its most ephemeral reigned supreme in the early part of the year: hands and feet decorated with painted-on henna patterns. Stars from Laurence Fishburne to Mira Sorvino sported the fade-able fad at gala events (and the Thursday night bowling league?).

24

Photography by **Robert Lewis**

1ST

FIRST QUARTERLY REPORT

New year, new hope. Naturally, we cast about for auspicious omens: Will the stars smile on us? No guarantees. For example, even before the traditional uplifting note could be sounded in the President's second Inaugural Address, the speaker of the House had admitted to violating his own institution's rules on ethics. An ongoing hostage crisis in Peru, a botched investigation into the death of a young beauty queen in Colorado, bombs exploding at a women's health clinic in Atlanta—hopeful signs seemed hard to come by. But after some searching ...

"To the degree I was too brash, too self-confident or too pushy, I apologize." —**Newt Gingrich,** after narrowly winning reelection as speaker of the House

"Next time I talk to Eleanor, I'll tell her you said hello." —**Hillary Clinton,** to reporter Bob Woodward, who had written that she had imaginary conversations with Mrs. Roosevelt

"I, Robert J. Dole, do solemnly swear…uh, sorry. Wrong speech." —**Bob Dole,** receiving the Presidential Medal of Freedom at the White House

"I want this man, and I want him convicted, and I want him sentenced, and I want him to go to jail." —**Camille Cosby,** after police arrested a suspect in the killing of her son, Ennis

"You dumb jerk. You must think we're fools." —Juror **Virginia Cruse,** on what went through her mind as she listened to O.J. Simpson's testimony at his civil trial

"Really, we're just like the Lions or the Elks. We want to be involved in the community." —**Jeff Coleman,** grand wizard of the Royal Knights of the Ku Klux Klan, on why the group should be allowed to adopt a highway in Florida

"I'm honored. There's no such thing as baa-aa-aa-d publicity." —**Dolly Parton,** singer and eponym of the first sheep clone

"There is still no cure for the
common birthday."
—**John Glenn,**
75, announcing his retirement from the Senate

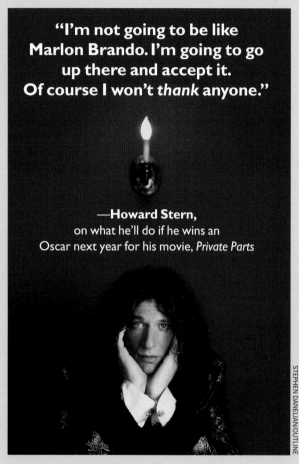

"**I'm not going to be like
Marlon Brando. I'm going to go
up there and accept it.
Of course I won't *thank* anyone.**"

—**Howard Stern,**
on what he'll do if he wins an
Oscar next year for his movie, *Private Parts*

STEPHEN DANELIAN/OUTLINE

"I see
hell in **hello.**
It's disguised by the *o*,
but once you see it, it will
slap you in the face."

—Texas flea market operator **Leonso Canales,**
on why he fought to have Kleberg County's official
courthouse greeting changed to *heaveno*

"What's wrong with
'Howdy, y'all'?"

—Texas bookseller **Madolyn Musick,**
on the decision to change the greeting to *heaveno*

Tamagotchi Fever!

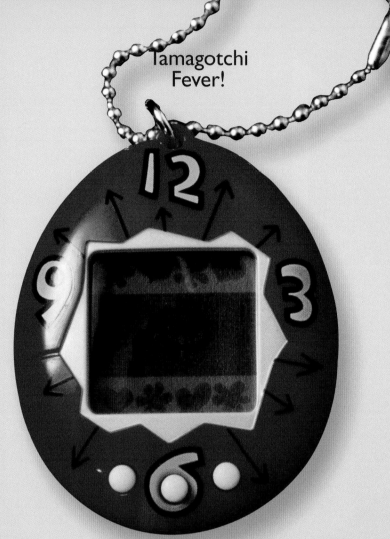

It cries, needs to be fed and cleaned up after
and doesn't sleep enough. Is this toy *too* real?

New Stamps

Philatelists and nonphilatelists alike can appreciate these: This year's crop
of postage stamps makes for great collecting and better-looking snail mail.
A sampling of the U.S. Postal Service's offerings—pretty botanicals, scary
movie monsters, ferocious dinosaurs and, for the first time ever, triangular
stamps—can be seen in each of
this book's Quarterly Reports.

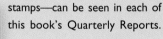

Show Me the Oscar, 1997

Best Picture
The English Patient

Best Actor
Geoffrey Rush, *Shine*

Best Actress
Frances McDormand, *Fargo*

Best Supporting Actor
Cuba Gooding Jr., *Jerry Maguire*

Cuba Gooding Jr., winner

Best Supporting Actress
Juliette Binoche, *The English Patient*

Best Adapted Screenplay
Billy Bob Thornton, *Sling Blade*

Best Original Screenplay
Joel and Ethan Coen, *Fargo*

Best Documentary Feature
When We Were Kings

Best Original Song
"You Must Love Me,"
Andrew Lloyd Webber
and Tim Rice, from *Evita*

Courtney Love, attendee

All-American Cheeseheads

Refreshing, these Green Bay Packers, with their Huck Finn quarterback, public stock offerings and leaps into the stands. Returning to the limelight via the Super Bowl, they came back in style—notwithstanding the headgear.

JAMES V. BIEVER

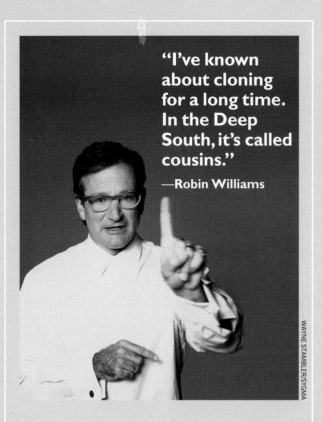

"I've known about cloning for a long time. In the Deep South, it's called cousins."
—Robin Williams

Jessie Lee Brown Foveaux

Rookie of the Year

This 98-year-old first-time author packed the punch of a Stephen King when she scooped up a million-dollar book contract for *The Life of Jessie Lee Brown from Birth up to 80 Years*. But she didn't get carried away: She planned to help her church; then "I might just get myself a new dress."

Three-Cornered Statement

The debut of triangular stamps in March was historic; a triumphant U.S. postmaster general was able to declare, "Stamps aren't square."

"You're No. 64. Welcome to the fraternity."
—former Secretary of State **Henry Kissinger,** to current Secretary Madeleine Albright

"Henry, it's no longer a fraternity."
—**Albright**

They Made Us Proud
Elizabeth Taylor

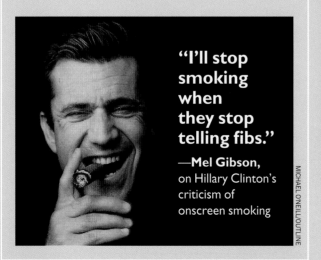

"I'll stop smoking when they stop telling fibs."
—**Mel Gibson,** on Hillary Clinton's criticism of onscreen smoking

When a legendary looker goes bald in public to help educate others about brain surgery, we applaud. When she lets her raven tresses grow out an all-natural white, we're inclined to let out a wolf whistle. Ms. Taylor proves that beauty is more than skin-deep.

THE JONBENÉT RAMSEY CASE

Mr. Ramsey,

Listen carefully! We are a group of individuals that represent a small foreign faction. We respect your bussiness but not the country that it serves. At this time we have your daughter in our pozession. She is safe and unharmed and if you want her to see 1997, you must follow our instructions to the letter.

You will withdraw $118,000.00 from your account. $100,000 will be in $100 bills and the remaining $18,000 in $20 bills. Make sure that you bring an adequate size attache to the bank. When you get home you will put the money in a brown paper bag. I will call you between 8 and 10 am tomorrow to instruct you on delivery. The delivery will be exhausting so I advise you to be rested. If we monitor you getting the money early, we might call you early to arrange an earlier delivery of the money and hence a earlier pick-up of your daughter.

Any deviation of my instructions will result in the immediate execution of your daughter. You will also be denied her remains for proper burial. The two gentlemen watching over your daughter do not particularly like you so I advise you not to provoke them. Speaking to anyone about your situation, such as Police, F.B.I., etc., will result in your daughter being beheaded. If we catch you talking to a stray dog, she dies. If you alert bank authorities, she dies. If the money is in any way marked or tampered with, she dies. You will be scanned for electronic devices and if any are found, she dies. You can try to deceive us but be warned that we are familiar with law enforcement countermeasures and tactics. You stand a 99% chance of killing your daughter if you try to out smart us. Follow our instructions and you stand a 100% chance of getting her back. You and your family are under constant scrutiny as well as the authorities. Don't try to grow a brain John. You are not the only fat cat around so don't think that killing will be difficult. Don't underestimate us John. Use that good southern common sense of yours. It is up to you now John!

Victory!
S.B.T.C

A full year after the strangled, beaten and perhaps sexually molested body of six-year-old beauty queen JonBenét Ramsey (above) was discovered in the basement of her Boulder, Colo., home, a killer was still on the loose. The investigation of this Christmas 1996 crime (a year later one neighbor reported that police had never interviewed her) was bungled from the beginning. Boulder District Attorney Alex Hunter eventually pointed to John and Patricia Ramsey (below) as "the focus" in the case. The wealthy couple denied any guilt in their daughter's death, hired a team of eight lawyers and offered a $100,000 reward for leads. A ransom note (left) found in the house was one of few pieces of solid evidence, but authorities have not identified its author. In August the Ramseys moved to Atlanta, to a home near JonBenét's grave (bottom). As 1997 ended, the case remained open, as did the question of justice.

GLORY ROAD

150 YEARS AFTER A HISTORIC MORMON ODYSSEY

THE SAINTS GO MARCHING IN—AGAIN.

SEARCHING FOR A PROMISED LAND

They retraced their ancestors' steps, many wearing the heavy shoes, trousers and dresses of the 19th century, pulling handcarts filled with their belongings, steering horse-drawn carriages or simply walking along the 1,000-mile trail. The three-month re-creation of the historic exodus of the Latter-day Saints from Omaha to Salt Lake City concluded this past July—150 years after the original journey's end. In 1847, Brigham Young looked about the Salt Lake Valley and declared to 148 followers, "This is the right place." The thousands of Mormons who took part in this summer's caravan agreed.

I REJOICE ALL THE TIME."
—MIDWIFE PATTY BARTLETT SESSIONS, 1847

EMBRACING
A LEGACY
OF COURAGE

In 1847, members of the Church of Jesus Christ of Latter-day Saints faced violent persecution for their beliefs and practices, then fearsome weather during their flight to freedom. In 1997, participants in the reenactment of the migration were greeted not by hostile enemies but by hospitable westerners (who invited weary walkers in for showers and community parties—including a polka fest); observers were filled with admiration for the Saints' adherence to faith and history. This modern trek was about both honoring the past and committing to the future: At least one young couple who met on the trail plan to marry.

LES STONE/SYGMA (2)

"I'M GOING TO GO HOME

AND I'M NEVER GOING TO FORGET THIS."
—SHAUNA DICKEN, GREAT-GREAT-GRANDDAUGHTER OF PATTY SESSIONS, 1997

APRIL
MAY
JUNE

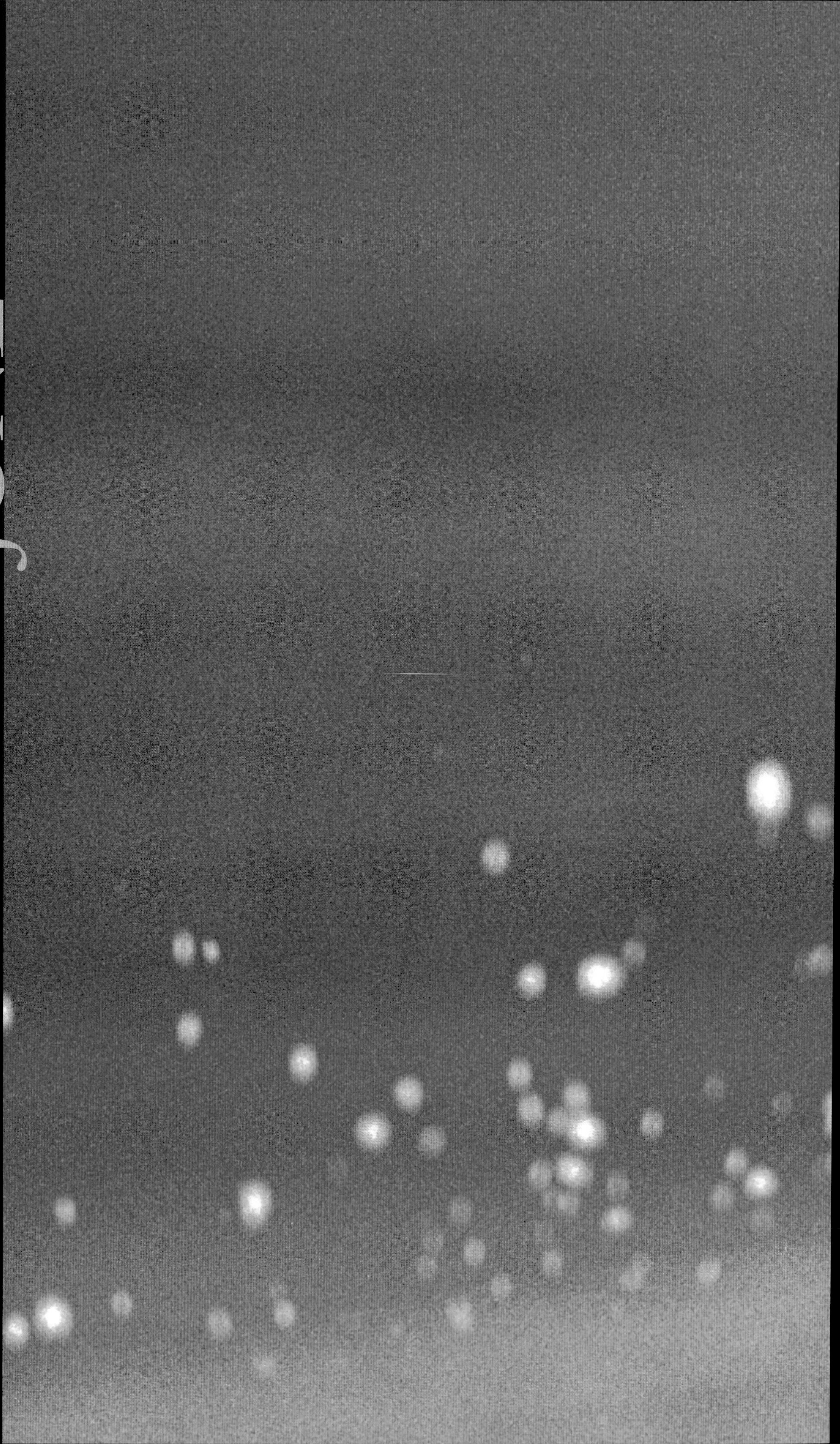

Burning Bright

He's 21, a gazillionaire, beyond talented—and he loves his mother and father! Tiger Woods, seen here just before winning the Masters Tournament with a record score of 270 (12 strokes ahead of the second-place finisher), proved that golf is no longer the sole provenance of middle-aged white men.

36

Four days into a 16-day mission, NASA decides to bring home the space shuttle *Columbia* because of **a power supply problem.** An emergency landing is ruled out, however, as the crew's safety is not immediately threatened. Since space shuttle flights began in 1981, only two other missions have ended early, also because of equipment failure.

Among the 20 Pulitzer Prize–winners is trumpeter and composer **Wynton Marsalis,** 35. His *Blood on the Fields,* one of the works that drew the attention of the prize jury, is a jazz oratorio tracing the journey of an African couple sold into slavery in the United States.

In a unanimous decision, a federal appeals court upholds the constitutionality of California's Proposition 209—**an anti–affirmative action initiative.** President Clinton, an opponent of 209, says affirmative action supporters will have to "regroup and find new ways to achieve the same objective."

Twist and Shout

Miami residents have weathered crime waves, heat waves and hurricanes, but even the most seasoned Floridians were taken by surprise when a freak tornado whistled through town. In a few terrifying moments it uprooted trees, snapped light poles and shattered windows— then moved on.

39

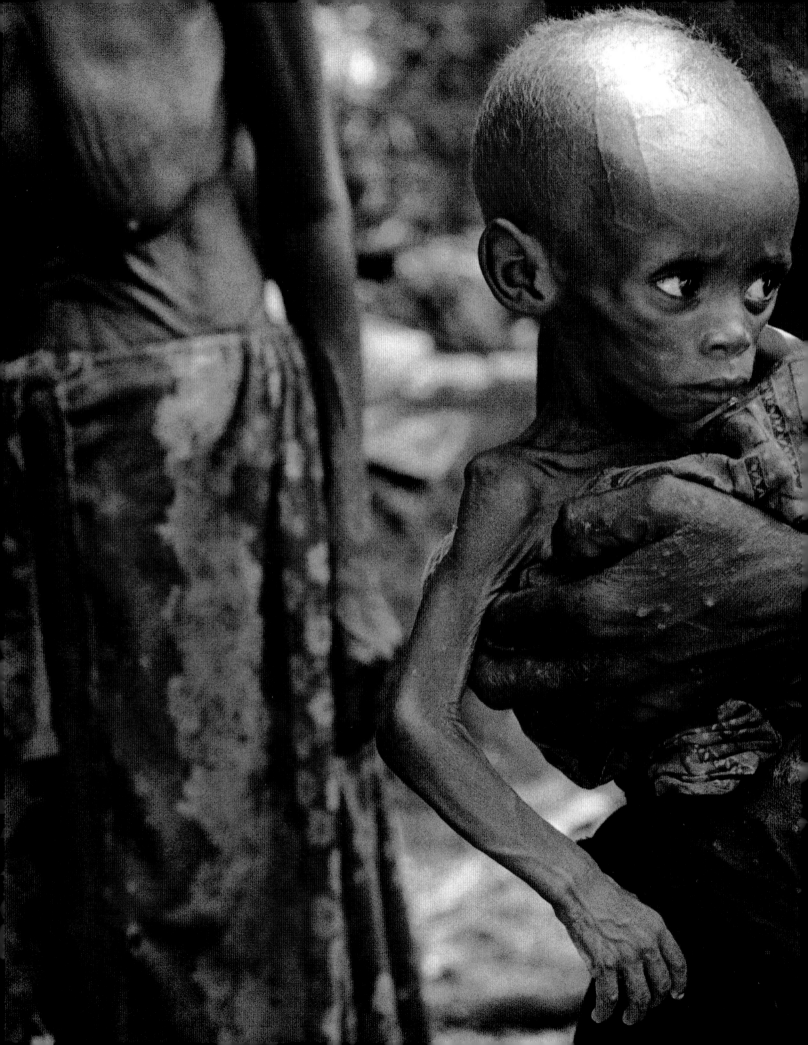

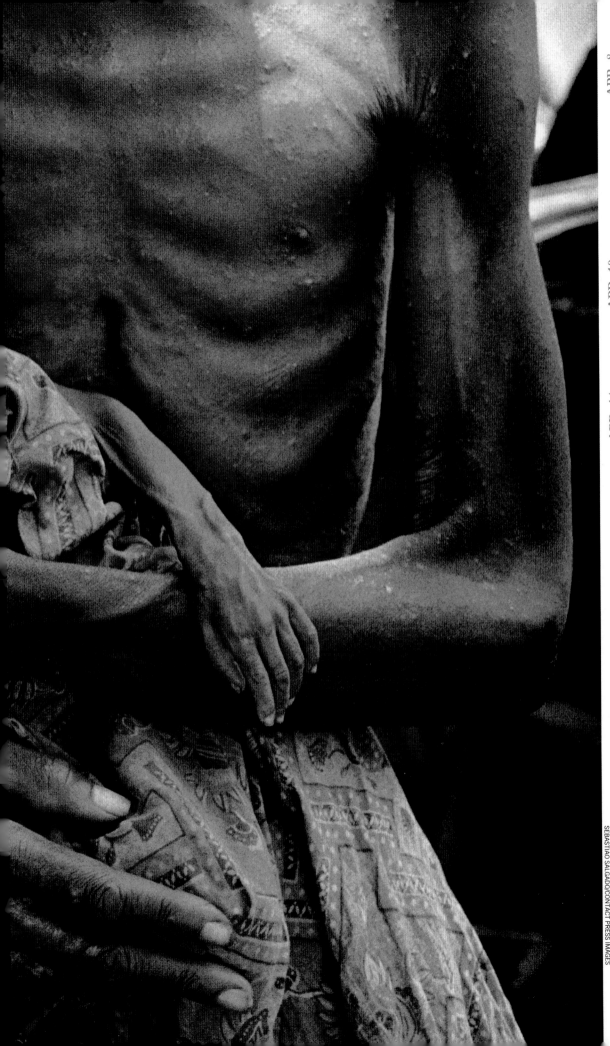

APR. 8 A study confirms what many doctors had suspected: Girls are beginning puberty earlier than was previously thought. Girls **as young as age seven** are showing signs of sexual maturing, with African American females ahead of white girls by about a year. Along with race and ethnicity, determining factors include nutrition and environment.

APR. 10 Ten thousand **welfare recipients will be hired,** the President says, by the federal government. Over the next four years, entry-level jobs—including six at the White House—are to be filled by former welfare recipients.

APR. 14 Actress Ellen DeGeneres makes a very public outing: herself. Two weeks later her TV character, Ellen Morgan, also reveals her homosexuality. **The "coming out" episode** of *Ellen,* featuring guest appearances by Melissa Etheridge, k.d. lang, Laura Dern and Oprah Winfrey, scores the series its highest-ever ratings.

A Deadly March

In 1994, hundreds of thousands of Rwandans fled to Zaire to escape the troubles of their own country. In the past three years they have found only misfortune: widespread famine, local rebel troops who despise them, civil war and no safe way home. This baby, photographed in April, knows nothing of the political tangles that have deprived him of shelter, food and hope for the future.

41

APR. 14 James B. McDougal, the Whitewater business partner of Bill and Hillary Clinton, is sentenced to three years in prison. Though **convicted on 18 felony counts,** his cooperation with the investigation spares him harsher punishment.

APR. 17 Speaker Newt Gingrich announces he will borrow $300,000 from former Senate Majority Leader Bob Dole to **pay the fine** levied by the House ethics committee. Dole, who offered the money after Gingrich had explored other options—such as using legal defense funds—says his loan is intended to "help the party and help Newt."

APR. 24 Opening statements in the trial of Oklahoma City bombing suspect Timothy McVeigh are heard. Held in Denver, **the trial begins** nearly two years to the day after the blast that killed 168 people. Security around the courthouse is tight.

Rite of Passage

At one stroke after midnight on June 30, the British colony of Hong Kong was transferred back to Communist China. More than 4,000 troops of the People's Liberation Army, seen here during a farewell ceremony, formally reclaimed it. Chinese President Jiang Zemin reassured us: "One country, two systems." But the rest of the world watches closely.

APR. 25 *The Boston Globe* reports that Michael Kennedy, a son of Ethel and the late Robert F. Kennedy, had a five-year affair with his children's babysitter—**starting when she was 14.** A statutory rape investigation will be halted (the victim refuses to press charges) in July, and in August, Michael's older brother, Joseph P. Kennedy II, will drop his campaign for the Massachusetts governorship. Joe—whose own ex-wife has been challenging his attempts to annul their marriage—will cite "personal and family pressures."

APR. 27 Armed members of a militant fringe group known as the Republic of Texas take two hostages described as "prisoners of war." The group considers the state of Texas an independent nation, and its leader says, "**We are at war** with the United Nations and all foreign entities . . . not with the American people, but with the federal agencies, which have no jurisdiction here." The standoff is resolved a week later; one separatist flees, one is killed, the rest surrender.

Mission Accomplished

For the 71 hostages held for four months by Marxist guerrillas in the Japanese ambassador's residence in Lima, Peru, it started as just another day in captivity. But 10 minutes after the hostages were secretly warned, military commandos blasted into the compound through underground tunnels in a brilliantly executed raid. One hostage, two commandos and all 14 guerrillas died in the rescue.

APR. 28 Human remains found at the crash site of a downed Air Force jet near Eagle, Colo., are identified as those of the pilot, Capt. Craig Button. The plane, missing since Button inexplicably veered off course during a routine training mission on April 2, had been carrying **four 500-pound bombs.** Conspiracy theories flourish but are completely unsubstantiated.

APR. 30 The White House announces that the First Daughter will break with the family tradition of East Coast colleges: Chelsea will head to California's Stanford University in the fall. President **Clinton is philosophical:** "Well, the planes run out there, and the phones work out there, and the E-mail works out there, so we'll be all right."

MAY 2 Flamboyant businessman **Donald Trump** and his second wife, Marla Maples, announce they will separate after three and a half years of marriage. The couple have one child, four-year-old Tiffany.

Love's Labour Won

Tony Blair (fourth from left) pulled up a seat at the pub before his win as England's new prime minister ended 18 years of Conservative rule. The Labour leader with the Kennedy hair and the Clinton moves quickly renewed peace negotiations with the IRA and helped the royal family with some much-needed media savvy following the death of Princess Diana. His approval rating? Through the roof.

46

MAY 6 Basketball's Rick Pitino becomes the highest-paid professional sports coach in history when the Boston Celtics sign him for **$70 million over 10 years.** Also in May: Former Celtics superstar Larry Bird, 40, accepts his first coaching job—another multimillion-dollar deal—with the Indiana Pacers.

MAY 10 Three *Seinfeld* cast members settle with NBC for $600,000 apiece per episode. Julia Louis-Dreyfus (Elaine), Jason Alexander (George) and Michael Richards (Kramer) had **threatened to quit** unless they were paid $1 million per episode—the salary of the show's star, Jerry Seinfeld. The 1997-98 season, the show's ninth, is rumored to be its last.

MAY 14 After months of international debate, Russia reluctantly agrees to an **eastward expansion** of the North Atlantic Treaty Organization, the 47-year-old military alliance. The new members will be Poland, the Czech Republic, Hungary and other European nations left behind the Iron Curtain.

You Go, Girl

They came, they saw, they cheered. Skeptics had wondered how many people would turn out for the WNBA's June debut, but ticket sales far outstripped expectations. Young girls with new attitudes filled the seats to root for instant stars like Cynthia Cooper of the Houston Comets, here scoring a blow against the New York Liberty—and for women's sports.

48

DAVID E. KLUTHO/SPORTS ILLUSTRATED

MAY 15–24 The space shuttle *Atlantis* docks with Russia's trouble-plagued **orbiting space station, *Mir,*** and unloads urgently needed equipment. The mission also includes a personnel exchange: American astronaut Michael Foale replaces compatriot Jerry Linenger, who has been on board the damaged *Mir* for 122 days.

MAY 16 After seven months of guerrilla rebellion, Zairean leader Mobutu Sese Seko's 32-year reign is overthrown: **Rebel leader Laurent Kabila** declares himself head of state and changes the country's name to the Democratic Republic of the Congo.

MAY 20 *Monday Night Football* commentator Frank Gifford, 66, is pictured in the *Globe* with a former flight attendant whom the tabloid reportedly paid to rendezvous with Gifford at a New York City hotel. Both he and his wife, **Kathie Lee Gifford,** decide not to discuss the scandal publicly.

Brave New World

As part of an ongoing experiment to study brain damage in human babies, Japanese researchers created an artificial uterus made of Plexiglas. This 125-day-old goat fetus, sleeping peacefully in faux utero, received oxygen and nutrients from manmade umbilical cords. The birth process? Researchers simply removed it from the tank.

PETER MIKELBANK

MAY 22 First Lieutenant Kelly Flinn, 26, America's first female B-52 pilot, accepts a general discharge from the Air Force (preferring that to facing a court-martial) for charges stemming from an adulterous affair with a civilian. Public discussion focuses on **the military's double standard,** forcing closer scrutiny of adulterous men in the service. Following Flinn's dismissal, two male Army generals will retire rather than risk facing similar charges.

MAY 24 In an upset vote, Mohammed Khatami, a candidate who stands for social reform and tolerance, is elected president of Iran. He is **supported by millions** of Iranians who are frustrated by the encroachment of Islamic law on their government.

MAY 27 United States Representative Susan Molinari surprises everyone when she announces she will leave Congress to become an anchor on *CBS News Saturday Morning.* The move particularly puzzles political leaders, who consider the **39-year-old Republican** (and keynote speaker at her party's national convention in San Diego last year) a likely comer.

The Usual Suspects

Hollywood glitzerati, Euro auteurs and scantily clad starlets converged on the south of France to celebrate the 50th birthday of the Cannes film festival in May. The paparazzi swarmed as stars like Sean Penn, Robin Wright Penn and John Travolta glammed it up. "I'm going to see everyone that won't work with me," Sylvester Stallone announced. "I can't wait."

53

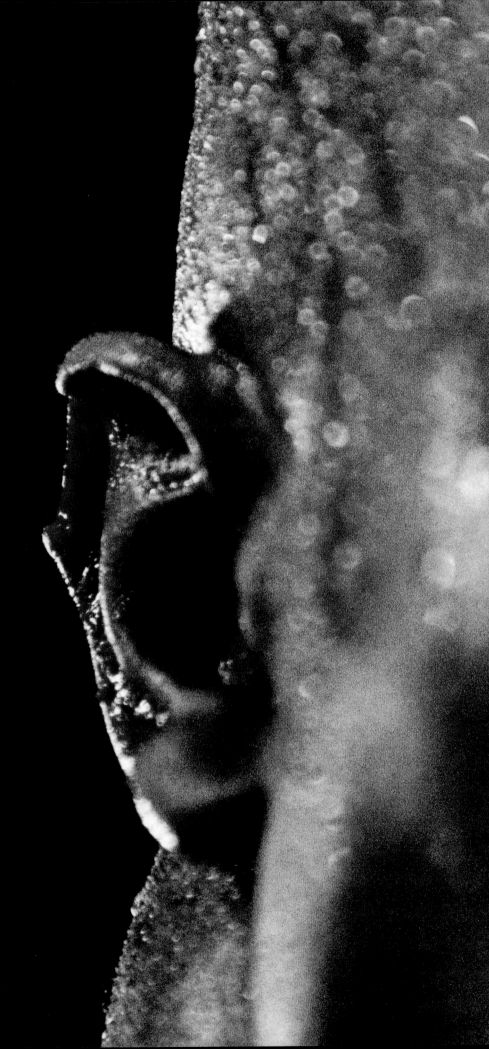

MAY 27 A boon for Paula Jones: The Supreme Court rules that her sexual harassment suit against President Clinton can proceed. The **high court's unanimous decision**—that sitting Presidents can be held liable for their actions outside of their official duties—sets a precedent. The case stems from an alleged incident while Clinton was governor of Arkansas.

MAY 28 The Federal Trade Commission charges R.J. Reynolds Tobacco Co. with a federal violation for using Joe Camel—the company's cartoon mascot—to **market cigarettes to minors.** The agency seeks to ban Joe Camel's image from settings where children might see it but allows Reynolds to use the character on advertisements in adult venues, such as bars.

JUNE 5 Harold Nicholson, the highest-ranking CIA officer ever **convicted of espionage,** is sentenced to 23 years and seven months in prison. He says his plan was to spend the $300,000 he was paid—for selling secrets to Russia—on his children, to make up "for the long hours at work."

Raging Bull

Billed as "the Sound and the Fury," it quickly became known as "Bite Night." Mike Tyson lost it in the third round of his Las Vegas heavyweight championship rematch in June and bit both of Evander Holyfield's ears. The first time he was warned, the second time he was disqualified. Later he was fined $3 million and had his boxing license revoked.

55

JAMSHID BAIRAMI/AFP

A New Jersey teenager gives birth to a baby boy in a bathroom stall, then apparently **leaves the infant to die** in a trash can before returning to her senior prom. The act is one in a recent series of teens concealing pregnancies and later killing or abandoning their newborns. The disturbing trend provokes a panel discussion organized by a group called Post-Partum Support International: Experts conclude that many girls fear revealing pregnancies, particularly to their mothers.

Mets vs. Yankees? Cubs vs. White Sox? Baseball history is made when National League teams face American League teams for the first time during the regular season. **Interleague baseball** will be tested for two years in an attempt to heighten fans' interest in the sport.

Timothy McVeigh, 29, having been found guilty of setting off the truck bomb that killed 168 people in Oklahoma City in 1995, is **sentenced to death.** The jury came to its unanimous decision after 11 hours of deliberation. As the verdict is read in the courtroom, the criminal mouths to his family, "It's O.K."

Earthquake in Iran

It measured 7.1 on the Richter scale, and the consequences were devastating. This dead child, being placed by her mother beside other casualties, was one of 2,400 Iranians who died; 50,000 were left homeless. Officials estimated the cost of rebuilding from this and a previous quake at $100 million, but some damage can never be repaired.

e4 c6 2. d4 d5 3. Nc3 dxe4

JUNE 14 Michael Jordan leads the Chicago Bulls to their fifth National Basketball Association championship title. Battling the flu in game five, MVP **Jordan performs the impossible** yet again by scoring 38 points. The Bulls go on to beat the Utah Jazz in a seven-game series.

JUNE 20 A proposed deal is reached between the nation's leading tobacco companies and the attorneys general of 40 states. **If it is ratified,** the manufacturers will pay the states $368.5 billion over 25 years toward the health care costs of patients with smoking-related illnesses. Tough restrictions on advertising are also suggested.

JUNE 25 The Swiss Bankers Association agrees to publish a list of the foreign names on unclaimed accounts opened before the end of World War II. **The dormant accounts,** worth some $42 million, are thought to have belonged to Holocaust victims.

JUNE 25 As a symbol of her embarkation on **a new life,** Diana, Princess of Wales, offers 79 of her cocktail dresses and evening gowns to Christie's for auction. The proceeds from the sale will benefit AIDS and cancer charities.

Am I Blue?

Man met microchip—and this time he lost. World chess champion Garry Kasparov looked all too human in a match against IBM's Deep Blue computer in New York in May. Although he won at their 1996 meeting, he lost the final game of this six-game match in only 19 moves. Kasparov wants a rematch; the computer is considering its options.

59

If we could keep love in a bottle, is this what it would look like? In 1997, Beanie Babies triggered spells of snuggling, swapping and die-trying shopping.

2ND

SECOND QUARTERLY REPORT

Some years seem to crawl, some to fly; 1997 broke the sound barrier. Before we'd recovered from the snows that swept much of the country, they had melted into devastation, especially in soon-to-be-famous Grand Forks, N. Dak. (page 66). One thing that seemed to move slower than molasses was the endless buildup to the coming-out (finally!) of Ellen DeGeneres in *Time* and on her sitcom. Yada, yada, yada.

"He heard about the idea of my playing him. He looked me up and down and finally said, 'You almost as pretty as me.'"
—**Will Smith,** on meeting Muhammad Ali

"...there's nothing wrong with you, and don't let anyone make you ashamed of who you are."
—**Ellen DeGeneres**, addressing gay teenagers while accepting a writing Emmy for her show, *Ellen,* in which her character came out as a lesbian

"I really thought I'd be seeing Elvis soon."
—**Bob Dylan,** on his bout with a potentially fatal infection

"He would say to me, 'You are so smart; why do you believe in God?' And I'd say, 'You are so smart; why don't you believe in God?'"
—**Rev. Joan Brown Campbell,** recalling the author and astronomer Carl Sagan at a memorial service

"If you hear of me getting married, slap me."
—**Elizabeth Taylor,** to Barbara Walters on *20/20*

"Just two people, that's all, and we ended adultery in Kandahar forever. Even 100,000 police could not have the effect that we achieved with one punishment of this kind."
—**Alhaj Maulavi Qalamuddin,** head of the ruling Taliban's General Department for the Preservation of Virtue and Prevention of Vice, on the stoning to death of two people accused of adultery in Afghanistan last year

"I *am* worried about my old fans' reactions. But most of them are dead."
—**Pat Boone,** on his new album of heavy-metal standards

"My heart looks like that building did. It has a huge hole."

—**Diane Leonard,** whose husband was killed in the Oklahoma City bombing

> **"If the court please, I wish to use the words of Justice Brandeis ... to speak for me. He wrote, 'Our government is the potent, the omnipresent teacher. For good or for ill, it teaches the whole people by its example.'"**
>
> —**Timothy McVeigh,** at his sentencing hearing

Nine Lives, Seven Tonys

On June 19, *Cats* set a new Broadway record (displacing *A Chorus Line*) for longevity: 6,138 performances. And 225 gallons of makeup remover used thus far.

Rookie of the Year

Hideki Irabu

Dubbed the Orient Express, this Japanese pitcher was signed by the Yankees, debuted impressively, then fizzled, big-time. Bounced to the minors, the six-footer also known as Headache-y still had his $12.8 million contract to keep him warm.

"He's Moses to our people. I'm serious."

—**Wayne Lapierre,** of the National Rifle Association, after actor Charlton Heston was elected first vice president

"The right to keep and bear arms is the one right that allows rights to exist at all."

—**Charlton Heston**

Not Quite Fitting?

Practicing the politics of inclusion, Mattel introduced Barbie's handicapped friend, Share a Smile Becky, who—as it turned out—couldn't squeeze into the elevator in Barbie's Dream House. A little retooling is in the works.

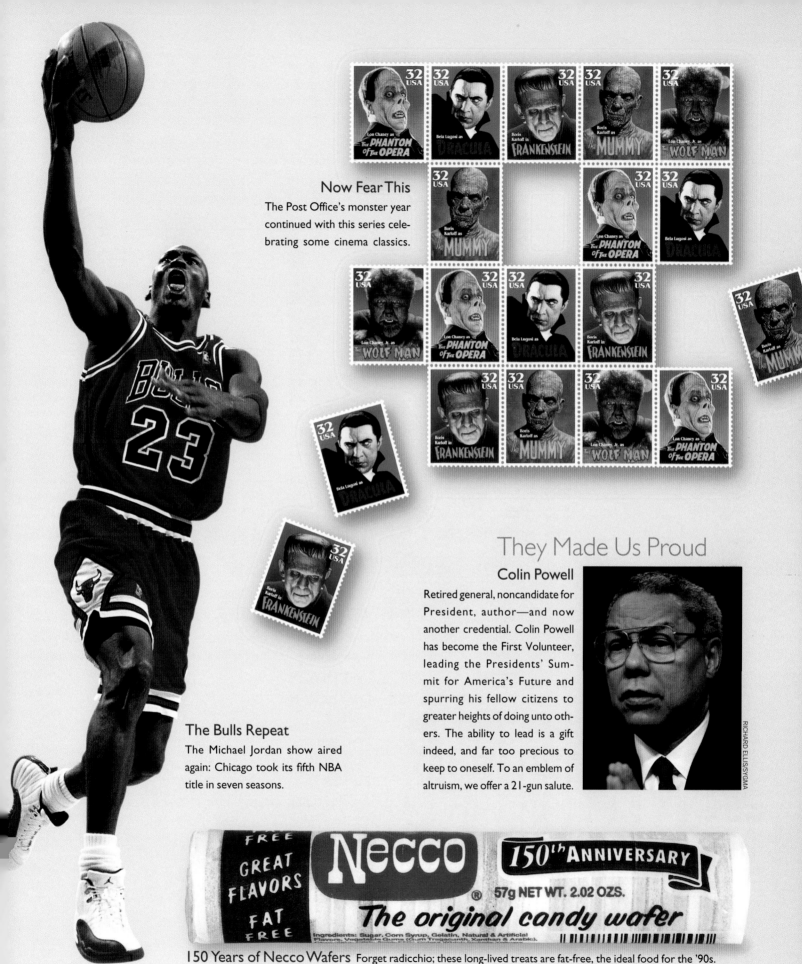

Now Fear This

The Post Office's monster year continued with this series celebrating some cinema classics.

The Bulls Repeat

The Michael Jordan show aired again: Chicago took its fifth NBA title in seven seasons.

They Made Us Proud

Colin Powell

Retired general, noncandidate for President, author—and now another credential. Colin Powell has become the First Volunteer, leading the Presidents' Summit for America's Future and spurring his fellow citizens to greater heights of doing unto others. The ability to lead is a gift indeed, and far too precious to keep to oneself. To an emblem of altruism, we offer a 21-gun salute.

RICHARD ELLIS/SYGMA

150 Years of Necco Wafers Forget radicchio; these long-lived treats are fat-free, the ideal food for the '90s.

THE BIG FIVE-O

Baby boomers—those born during the postwar years, when industry (and parents) was rolling out product in big numbers—began celebrating the half century mark last year. Now that it's begun, there's no stopping it: Until the year 2014, a good-size batch of boomers will turn 50 each year. For 1997 that distinction goes to aging rock stars and other icons.

Kareem Abdul-Jabbar
Meredith Baxter
Johnny Bench
David Bowie
Tom Clancy
Hillary Rodham Clinton
Jane Curtin
Ted Danson
Danny Glover
Arlo Guthrie
Emmylou Harris
Elton John

The Howdy Doody Show (1)
Say, kids, what time is it? A half century after Buffalo Bob's debut.

Stephen King
Kevin Kline
David Letterman
Iggy Pop
Dan Quayle
Nolan Ryan
Pat Sajak
Arnold Schwarzenegger
O.J. Simpson
Steven Spielberg
Danielle Steel
Cheryl Tiegs
Ron Wood

Billy Crystal (2)
His movies haven't been great lately, but who cares? As Oscar Emcee Numero Uno, he's a national treasure.

Ajax (3)
Also 50 this year: Ajax, the foaming cleanser; the Marshall Plan; the transistor; and Levittown.

Goodnight Moon (4)
Generations have been lulled to sleep by this nursery classic. "Goodnight moon. Goodnight air. Goodnight noises everywhere."

GOODNIGHT MOON
by Margaret Wise Brown
Pictures by Clement Hurd

6

Jackie Robinson (6)

This year the major leagues retired the number 42. The memory of the giant who broke baseball's color barrier in 1947 remains.

Glenn Close (7)

Still fatally attractive despite her affection for spotted fur, Close marked her fiftieth year with a ride in *Air Force One*.

Matisse's *Jazz* (8)

A great artist, a pair of scissors, colored paper. First published in 1947, *Jazz* is still cutting-edge.

Sno Balls (9)

They've been on *The X-Files* and on the space shuttle *Columbia*. They're historic, right? So eat up.

Farrah Fawcett (10)

We remember her as one of *Charlie's Angels*, and that darn poster keeps popping into our heads.

7

8

9

10

50 YEARS AGO

Indian Independence
The world's largest democracy emerged from British rule.

The CIA
The new spy agency replaced the Office of Strategic Services.

Frederick's of Hollywood
Mail-order naughties appeared.

The Royal Marriage
Philip and Elizabeth were wed.

"WE WILL REBUILD,
AND WE WILL
BE STRONGER,
AND WE WILL
BE IN IT TOGETHER."
— Grand Forks Mayor Pat Owens

FORCES OF
NATURE

Red River Ruins
The fire that gutted part of
downtown Grand Forks—
caused by "the Flood of the
Century"—raged for two days:
Fire trucks could not negotiate
the city's four feet of near-
freezing muddy water.

67

"ONE DAY I HAVE A HOME, AND THE NEXT DAY I DON'T.... YOU'D SEE OTHER DISASTERS AND NOT KNOW HOW THOSE PEOPLE FELT. WHEN IT HITS HOME, YOU KNOW. "

As the battle of man vs. nature unfolded in the Red River valley, nature appeared to be winning hands down. Winter blizzards blew deadly windchills and continued to dump snow well into April. When the snow melted, the Red River rose. Residents of Grand Forks, N.Dak., and neighboring East Grand Forks, Minn., fought back fiercely, only to see the river rise to 54 feet, two feet above the highest dike. But the exhausted evacuees never admitted defeat. President Clinton spoke for many when he said, "We are proud to be Americans when we see what you have done in the face of this terrible disaster."

Deeper and Deeper
A commuter bus lies in Grand Forks, sideswiped by the flooding. The water had crested three days earlier, forcing all 8,000 residents of East Grand Forks and more than 90 percent of Grand Forks's 50,000 people to evacuate. Most would remain homeless for nearly a month.

Sweeping Solidarity

The river finally began to recede April 23, leaving damage estimated at more than $1 billion. Residents came together again, sweeping out devastated shops, homes and churches.

ERICA BERGER

Once electricity and plumbing were finally restored and evacuees were permitted back into what was left of their homes, the term "spring cleaning" took on new meaning: Inoperable appliances, shattered furniture, mud-drenched pianos and unwearable clothes—including ruined prom dresses and tuxedos—were carted to the dump by the ton. But to the astonishment of the rest of the nation, there was little complaining in the Red River valley. "We got out with our lives; the rest is just stuff," explained one survivor. Residents thanked an anonymous donor (later revealed to be McDonald's heiress Joan Kroc), who pledged $2,000 to each evacuated family, and gracefully accepted donations—including prom dresses—from neighbors near and far. The prom, like the people of Grand Forks, went on.

A Tragic Love Story

Millions of admirers around the world shared their sorrow over the loss of Princess Diana, a woman they loved from afar. It was sad to see her former husband called to Paris to bring home the body of a woman whom he never seemed to understand or care for enough. But the heart broke most for the true loves of her life: sons William, 15, and Harry, then 12.

FIONA HANSON/PA NEWS

72

JULY 5 Martina Hingis, 16, of Switzerland becomes the **youngest champion at Wimbledon** in 100 years, beating Jana Novotna of the Czech Republic. The next day, American Pete Sampras, 26, will defeat France's Cedric Pioline for his fourth Wimbledon title.

JULY 7 More than 40,000 believers begin a weeklong celebration in Roswell, N.Mex., to mark the 50th anniversary of a **supposed UFO landing.** For ufologists, lectures at the commemorative event cover topics such as alien abductions and human-alien hybrids.

JULY 9 Newer! Still voluntary! Most of the major networks agree to an expanded version of **the ratings system** instituted at the start of the year. Letters standing for elements of a show's content (for example, V for violence or L for profane language) will be added to the designations agreed upon earlier.

Young Again

She's been called *Old Ironsides* since a sailor noticed in 1812 that cannonballs seemed to bounce off her sides, but the USS *Constitution* is really made of oak. To mark the end of a lengthy restoration project—and her 200th birthday—the trusty battleship set sail under her own power this summer for the first time since 1881.

JULY 11 The scientific journal *Cell* releases a study confirming that modern humans never interbred with—and therefore **do not descend from—Neanderthals.** The finding comes after a groundbreaking test on a strip of DNA taken from the bone of a Neanderthal who lived 30,000 years ago.

JULY 12 Karenna Gore, 23, eldest daughter of the Vice President, weds a physician, Andrew Schiff, at Washington National Cathedral. Aretha Franklin provides the entertainment, and the bride is finally able to give up her **Secret Service code moniker,** "Smurfette."

JULY 13 The newly found remains of Ernesto "Che" Guevara are returned to Cuba, almost 30 years after **the Argentine guerrilla** was killed in Bolivia. Cuban President Fidel Castro will preside over a ceremony to honor his compatriot in the successful struggle to overthrow Cuba's former dictator Fulgencio Batista.

JULY 17 F.W. Woolworth Corp. announces it will close all 400 of its **five-and-dime stores** across the country. The 117-year-old chain finds that it can no longer compete with such giants as Wal-Mart, Kmart and Target.

Venus Rising

It was, until recently, strictly a family affair. Venus Williams, 17, who had been trained in seclusion by her father, hit the U.S. Open running. She became the first unseeded woman in the Open era to make it to the finals. There she lost to Martina Hingis, but we'll be seeing more of Venus. And her little sister, Serena, has a mean forehand too.

JULY 23 Andrew Cunanan, 27, the chief suspect in the murder of fashion designer Gianni Versace and four other men, is found dead on a Miami Beach houseboat, **an apparent suicide.** The hunt for Cunanan had involved more than 1,000 law enforcement agents across the country.

JULY 24 Alex Kelly, 30, is sentenced to 16 years in prison for the 1986 rape of a Connecticut teenager. **Kelly fled the country** on the eve of his trial in 1987 and spent eight years touring European resorts with his parents' support. In 1995 he surrendered to authorities in Switzerland and returned to the U.S. to face a jury.

JULY 25 Autumn Jackson, who claims that actor Bill Cosby is her father, is convicted of trying to **extort $40 million** from him. In an interview with Dan Rather after the murder of his son, Ennis, Cosby admitted to an affair with Jackson's mother some 20 years ago, but the question of paternity was not settled in the course of the trial, having been deemed by the presiding judge to be irrelevant to the extortion charges.

A Tyrant's Trial

He was the architect of the "killing fields," where more than a million Cambodians died by execution, torture and starvation. But in the end, it was Pol Pot's former Khmer Rouge comrades who staged a show trial, deep in the country's jungle. He claimed "my conscience is clear" but received a sentence of life imprisonment. Many thought he got off easy.

JULY 25 A Dallas jury awards $120 million in damages after finding that the local Roman Catholic diocese **covered up evidence** that a priest—Rev. Rudolph Kos—had sexually molested boys. The abuse occurred over a 15-year period, during which church officials reportedly received numerous warnings and complaints about Father Kos's misconduct.

AUG. 4 Ron Carey, president of the International Brotherhood of Teamsters, calls a strike by 185,000 unionized United Parcel Service workers after negotiations over pensions and the use of part-time workers falter. Since UPS normally handles four fifths of ground-shipped parcels, **the strike makes a shambles** of the U.S. package-delivery industry. Fifteen days later the two sides reach an accord and the conflict ends.

Flying High

In a rare occasion for celebration, thousands of Bosnians cheered divers during an international competition in July. The diving board extended from the ruins of an ancient Ottoman bridge destroyed during the 1992-95 war. In the following months unemployment, too, would soar—to 80 percent in some areas—and violence erupt again. But that would not take away the sweet freedom of this moment.

The oldest person in the world (according to official documents) dies at age 122. Jeanne Calment of Arles, France, appeared to be in good health near the time of her death, but the years finally took their toll. The French say she ate more than **two pounds of chocolate per week,** rode a bicycle until she was 100 and had quit smoking only five years before her demise.

A Korean Air Lines jumbo jet crashes as it approaches a runway on Guam, and 227 of the 254 onboard are killed. Most of the travelers were South Koreans— **vacationers and honeymooners**—and at least 13 were Americans. A broken glide slope indicator—a ground system that guides incoming planes—is considered a factor in the disaster.

Mourners' Tribute

To followers around the world she was known simply as Mother. When Mother Teresa died on September 5 in Calcutta at the age of 87, she was memorialized in a flowery portrait, as mourners massed to view her lying in state. The Roman Catholic nun's tireless work with the poor won her the Nobel Peace Prize in 1979. Her spirit won her hearts everywhere.

An alliance is formed **in the cyber world:** Microsoft will pay $150 million for a nonvoting stake in its rival, the struggling Apple. Faithful Macintosh users boo the deal when it is announced by Apple's interim CEO and cofounder, Steven P. Jobs, at a trade show. In the future, Apple machines will come preloaded with Microsoft's Internet Explorer Web browser, and Microsoft will develop Mac-compatible software.

Country and western megastar Garth Brooks ventures into alien territory, **playing a free concert** in New York City's Central Park. Surprise guest Billy Joel gets a standing ovation from the crowd of more than 250,000, as does Don McLean, who sings his "American Pie" with Brooks.

Go West, Young Girl

Just your average first day of school—not. But the First Family found plenty to laugh about at this college convocation as Chelsea Clinton started her freshman year at Stanford. Her temporary entourage consisted of Mom, Dad, Secret Service agents and some 200 reporters.

85

AUG. 10 Greg Maddux re-signs—for five years and $57.5 million—with the Atlanta Braves. The four-time Cy Young Award–winning pitcher is now the **highest-paid player in baseball.**

AUG. 14 Moments before being formally sentenced to death, Timothy McVeigh, the Oklahoma City bomber, **breaks the silence** he has maintained throughout his trial. He quotes Justice Louis D. Brandeis from a 1928 Supreme Court case: "He wrote: 'Our government is the potent, the omnipresent teacher. For good or for ill, it teaches the whole people by its example.' That's all I have."

AUG. 18 A jury in Louisiana finds that the Dow Chemical Company **willfully deceived women** by hiding information about the health risks of silicone used in breast implants. The decision is the first step in a four-phase trial, potentially involving the claims of 1,800 women.

A Silent Hunger

A deadly combination of flooding and drought has created a famine in North Korea that UNICEF estimates has left 80,000 children in danger of dying from starvation or disease. "The pantries are bare . . . hospital medicine cabinets are empty and the results could be catastrophic if these shortages are not eased by winter," warned Carol Bellamy, UNICEF's executive director, in August. Always, it seems, it is the youngest who are most at risk.

87

Hudson Foods—a meat supplier to Burger King, Safeway and Sam's Club—announces that it will close its Nebraska plant indefinitely and voluntarily recalls **25 million pounds of ground beef.** The company had already pulled more than one million pounds earlier in the month. The meat is thought to be contaminated by potentially deadly *E. coli* bacteria—a discovery made by Hudson Foods itself and then by the Agriculture Department. This is the largest recall in United States history.

Diana, Princess of Wales, 36, and her companion, Emad "Dodi" Fayed, are killed in a car crash in Paris. Passing through a tunnel, their Mercedes-Benz spins and smashes into a pillar. Paparazzi on motorcycles are immediately accused of causing the accident by chasing Diana's car. Later it will be determined that the driver, Henri Paul (who also died), was legally drunk when he took the wheel. (For a tribute to Diana, see pages 104 to 109.)

Ghost Town

Two years of worsening volcanic eruptions have left the tiny Caribbean island of Montserrat all but deserted. After 19 people died and entire villages were buried under volcanic ash, the former capital, Plymouth, was abandoned and the airport closed. By summer's end only 4,000 diehards still refused to leave paradise.

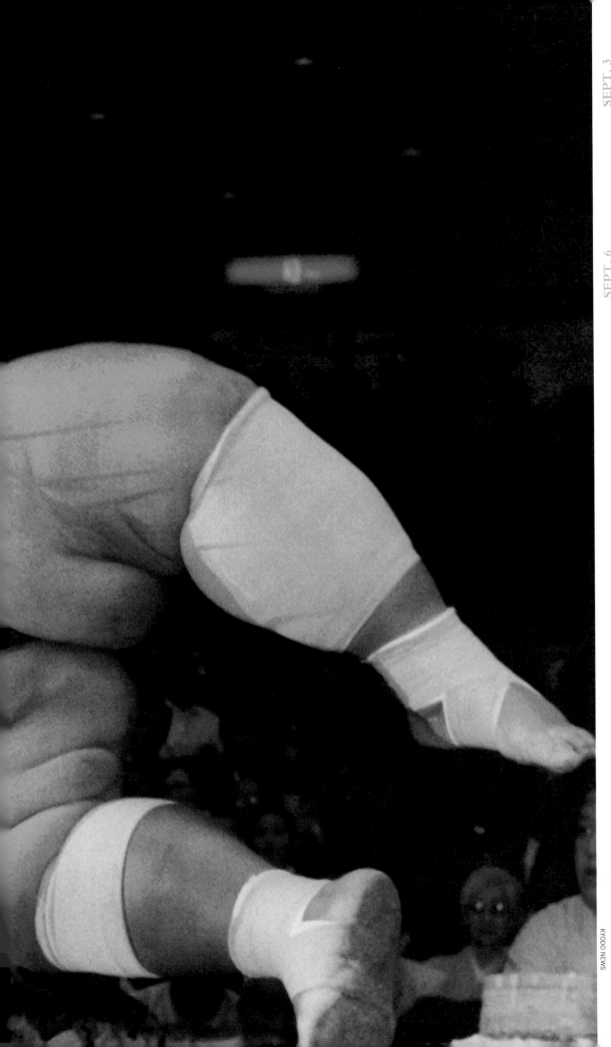

KYODO NEWS

SEPT. 3 Arizona Governor Fife Symington is convicted on seven felony counts for defrauding his lenders as a commercial real estate developer in the 1980s and early '90s. The **onetime rising star** of the Republican party, facing huge fines and possible prison time, is forced to resign. His sentencing is scheduled for early 1998.

SEPT. 6 Princess Diana is laid to rest in the Spencer family burial grounds outside of London. A million people line the streets of England's capital city as a **royal funeral** procession makes its way to Westminster Abbey; an estimated 30 million people in the U.S. and a record 31.5 million in Britain watch on television.

Weight Watchers

In a world of heavyweights, he takes the cake. At 605 pounds, Hawaiian-born sumo wrestling star Konishiki, seen here losing the Autumn Grand Sumo tournament in Tokyo, has gone overboard, even for this sport. He had to sit out part of the contest because of leg injuries owing to his enormous bulk.

91

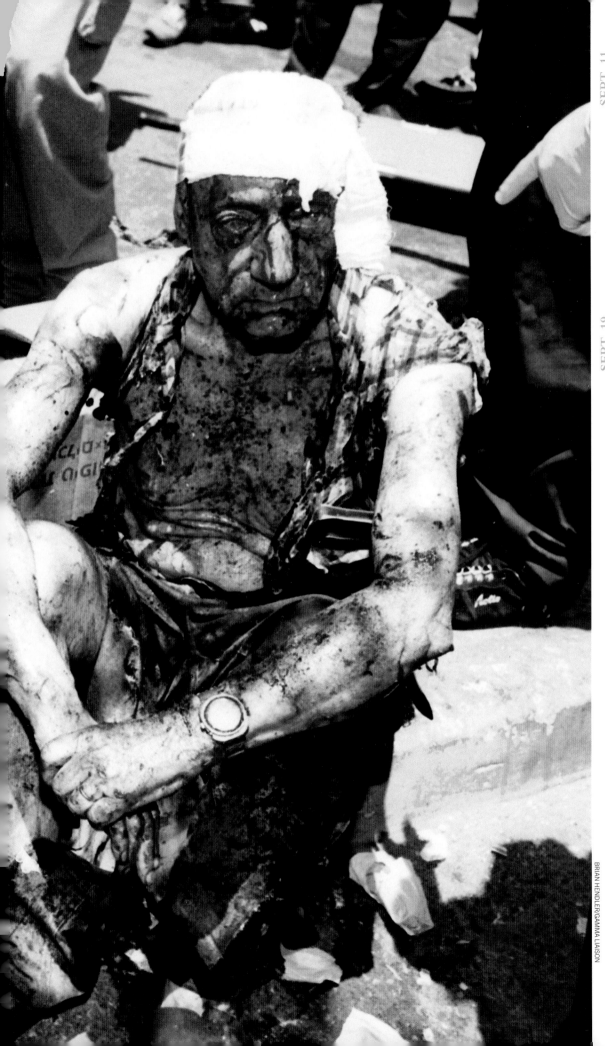

SEPT. 11 In its largest-ever investigation of sexual misconduct within its ranks, the Army reports that 47 percent of female soldiers polled had experienced "unwanted sexual attention," 15 percent had faced "sexual coercion," and 7 percent had been victims of sexual assault. Blaming "passive leadership" for **the persistence of sexual harassment** in the Army, the panel issues 10 recommendations to improve human relations.

SEPT. 19 Six military aircraft have crashed in unrelated accidents in a single week, killing 16 crew members. The Department of Defense responds by ordering the Air Force, Navy, Army and Marine Corps to **suspend all training flights** for a 24-hour period to review safety procedures. It has been found in the past that three out of every four military crashes are caused by human error.

The Terror, Again

The Jerusalem market was crowded with shoppers when two suicide bombers, members of the radical Islamic group Hamas, set off an explosion that killed them and 13 others and injured at least 150 more. While his country mourned, Prime Minister Benjamin Netanyahu told Palestinian leader Yasir Arafat, "I am not prepared to be satisfied with expressions of regret."

93

SEPT. 15 At the urging of the Food and Drug Administration, the makers of **two popular diet drugs** withdraw their products from the market. Fenfluramine (Pondimin) and dexfenfluramine (Redux)—often combined with phentermine, giving rise to the nickname fen-phen—may have caused heart valve damage in as many as 30 percent of the people in a test group.

SEPT. 18 Ted Turner, the billionaire vice chairman of Time Warner, pledges to United Nations agencies **a donation of up to $1 billion** over 10 years. The 58-year-old executive (whose personal net worth is $3.2 billion) says, "The world is just awash in money" and hopes his action will encourage philanthropy by other wealthy people.

SEPT. 24 The chief executive of Pepsico's $7.7 billion North American beverage business announces she is stepping down to spend more time with her family. Brenda Barnes, 43, **anticipating a negative reaction** from women in high-level jobs, says, "I hope people might say, 'Isn't it great that she could work so hard and make such a contribution to her company?'"

Red Rover

It was this summer's best rock festival. When the Pathfinder landed, with a few bounces, on Mars on July 4 and sent the foot-tall Sojourner out to explore the difficult terrain, millions followed along on the Internet. Despite a good deal of nail-biting, NASA has now proved that it is capable of operating a faraway vehicle by remote control.

95

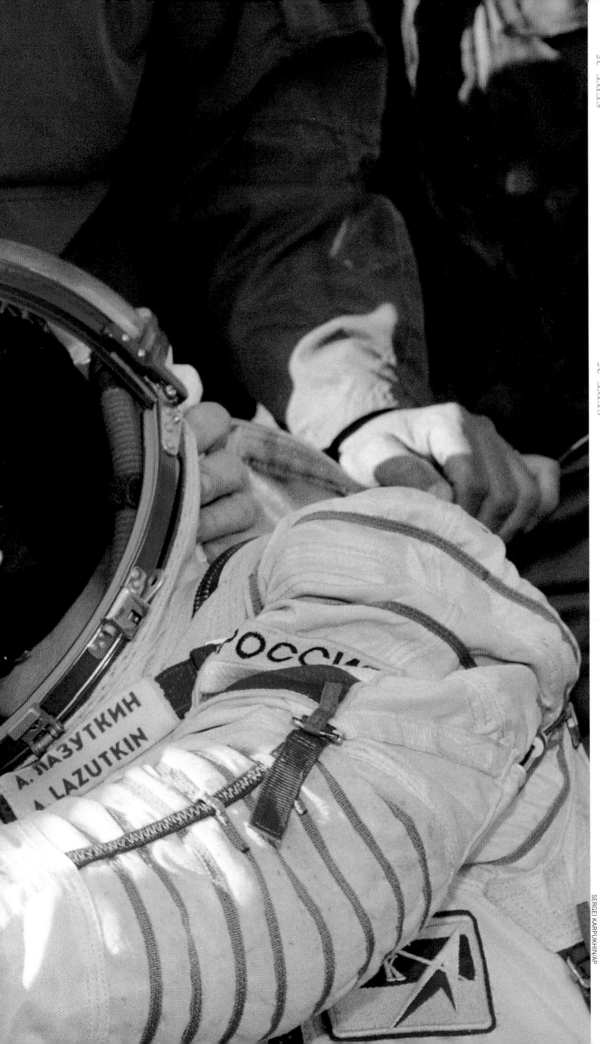

SEPT. 25 NBC sportscaster Marv Albert, 53, pleads guilty to charges of assault and battery. Hours later **the network fires him,** ending a seven-month ordeal that began when a 42-year-old Virginia woman accused Albert of biting her after her refusal to bring along another man to join them in a sexual encounter. As embarrassing details about his sex life are splashed across headlines, Albert pleads guilty to a reduced charge. The judge will later suspend sentencing, saying the conviction might be dropped if Albert honors a one-year probation.

SEPT. 25 The Little Rock Nine, a group of black high school students who chose to integrate the city's **all-white Central High School** in 1957, return to their alma mater to commemorate the event. Forty years ago, National Guard troops had to escort the students into and out of the school to protect them from jeering, violent crowds. This time they are honored by President Clinton.

Safe Landing

Having survived six months of near catastrophes on the 11-year-old space station *Mir,* Russian cosmonauts Vasili Tsibliyev and Alexander Lazutkin returned to Earth in August. Troubles onboard (fires, oxygen problems, even a deep-space crash) were so rampant that many Earth-bound spectators wondered if continuing this costly Russian-American venture was a mission impractical.

97

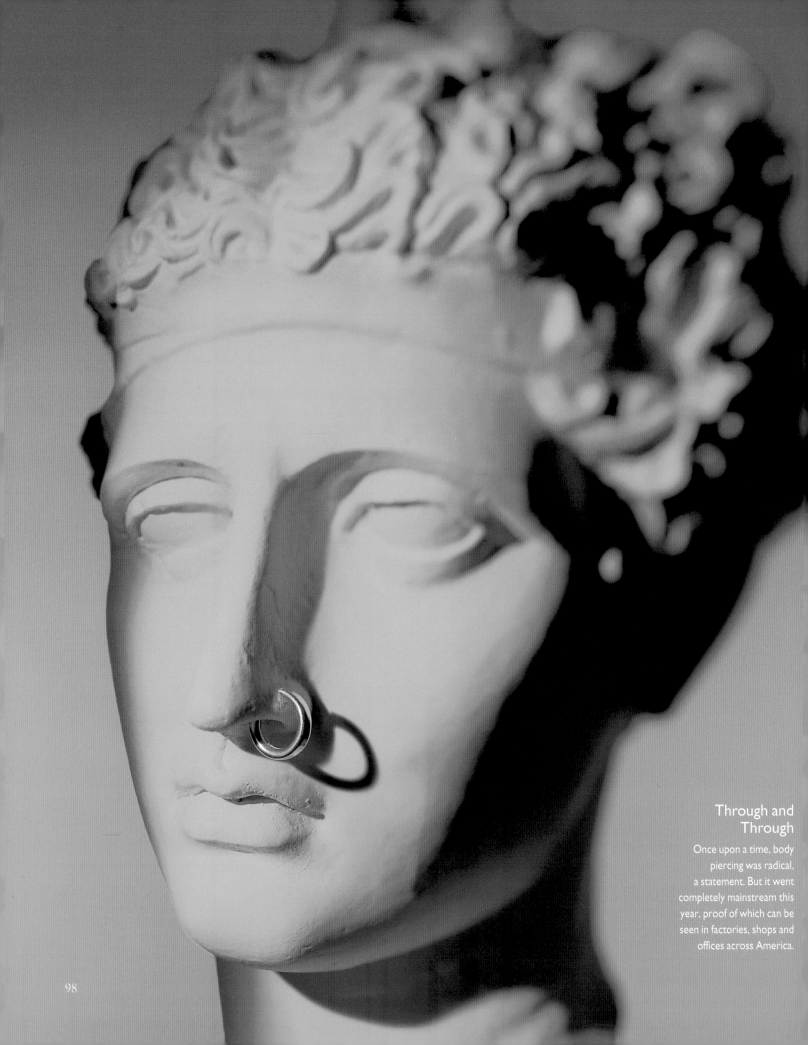

Through and Through

Once upon a time, body piercing was radical, a statement. But it went completely mainstream this year, proof of which can be seen in factories, shops and offices across America.

3RD

In the heat of summer, the pace slowed a bit. All the news seemed less urgent somehow. But it was just a warm-weather illusion: NATO was considering the greatest expansion in its history; campaign finance hearings that would haunt the Clinton administration were beginning; and, in a dazzling reminder of the nobility in our past, the USS *Constitution* sailed—soared?— under its own power for the first time in 116 years. Then, tragic eclipse: England lost her rose and India her Mother; the world mourned.

"I will be for you a father figure, but I am not your father."
—**Bill Cosby,** recalling what he once told Autumn Jackson, from court testimony given at her extortion trial

"He had the biggest heart of anyone in the building." —**Thurgood Marshall Jr.,** President Clinton's Cabinet secretary, on Justice William J. Brennan Jr.

"Almost everything I do in my private and personal life has been a part of the public record since I've been a very little boy. I don't think I've got a secret left."
—Massachusetts Rep. **Joseph Kennedy II,** citing recent family scandals in his decision not to run for governor

"He kills people."
—**Paul Philip,** of the FBI, when asked about Versace murderer Andrew Cunanan's modus operandi

"With every smell, I smell food. With every sight, I see food. I can almost hear food. I want to spade the whole lot through my mouth at Mach 2. Basta!" —**Sarah Ferguson,** Duchess of York, on temptations plaguing her during a vacation

"I'm sure he's very big back in his own country."
—**New York City policeman,** before Garth Brooks performed in Central Park

"If we wanted to get water from that glass over there, we beat it until it gave us water."
—**Ouk Vandath,** former Cambodian police officer, on how enforcement worked under Khmer Rouge rule

ROBERT LEWIS

99

HOT *now* DOUGHNUTS

"I'm definitely not a pioneer. That's for people like Jackie Robinson and Lee Elder. I'm just a product of their **hard work**."
—**Tiger Woods**

"I took it easy on him. I didn't want to go out there beatin' on the boy. So I let him take me by 26 strokes."
—**Will Smith,** on playing golf with Tiger Woods

KWAKU ALSTON/OUTLINE

"I always thought **it was boring**."
—Mets minor-league prospect **Ryan Jaroncyk,** on why he is retiring from baseball at the age of 20

"I thought **he was nuts**."
—**Melissa Raglin,** 12-year-old catcher for a Boca Raton, Fla., Little League team, on the umpire who asked if she wore a protective groin cup

Krispy Kremes

A wave of cholesterol swept the Smithsonian in July, when artifacts from the 60-year history of Krispy Kreme Doughnuts were accepted into the museum. Each store's no-holes-barred approach to fattening us up includes this neon sign—which lights up when a new batch is ready.

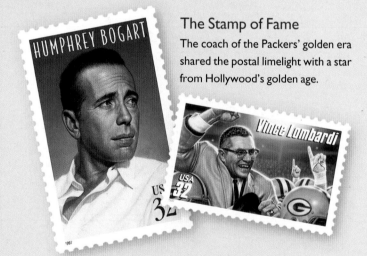

The Stamp of Fame

The coach of the Packers' golden era shared the postal limelight with a star from Hollywood's golden age.

Mike Foale Rookie of the Year

English-born (but all-American) astronaut Michael Foale spent 144 days of 1997 circling the earth every 90 minutes. The troubled *Mir* had a rough ride, but its challenges forged powerful bonds between Foale and his Russian fellow travelers. His breakthrough voyage was consistent with Foale's lifelong feeling that "if you don't explore, you might as well be a cabbage."

JOE MCNALLY

They Made Us Proud

Gladys Holm

Big woman (six feet tall), big heart. By copying her boss's stock trades on a small scale, the Illinois secretary amassed $18 million —then left it to Chicago's Children's Memorial Hospital. Holm died in 1996, but the hospital (where she was known to sick kids as the Teddy Bear Lady) did not make the bequest public until July of this year.

STEVE KELLEY/COPLEY NEWS SERVICE

Just Say No This boy may want to get it over with, but a study released in August suggested that kids ages six to nine who are spanked grow increasingly antisocial.

$542,506 The annual pension of former United Parcel Service CEO Kent Nelson, who retired in January with 30 years of service

$36,000 The average annual pension, under the new contract, for a UPS driver with 30 years of service

There are 3 billion women who don't look like supermodels and only 8 who do.

Worth Her Weight in Gold The Body Shop hung posters of the full-figured Ruby in their stores, with a tag line that speaks directly to 2,999,999,992 of us.

20 YEARS AGO

Saturday Night Fever

Does the new John Travolta want to be reminded of his star turn of 1977? It's all right. It's O.K. We can look the other way.

30 YEARS AGO

Twiggy

The British model arrived— what there was of her—in 1967, and we all just wanted to *feed* her. Funny how she no longer looks quite so odd.

40 YEARS AGO

The Cat in the Hat

What a mess he made! Hard to believe the good Dr. Seuss first foisted this, his greatest anarchist, upon us in 1957.

100 YEARS OF
DRACULA

Celebrations of the centennial of Bram Stoker's classic horror story ranged from an exhibit in Dublin to a weekend of vampiric revelry (with a graveyard procession) in Whitby, England; from the debut of an acclaimed ballet in Houston to a film series at New York's Museum of Modern Art. At a scholarly conference–fan convention in L.A., the guest of honor himself arrived by hearse and rose from his coffin to open the festivities. Presumably, the blood flowed freely

Max Schreck, 1922

Christopher Lee, 1958

Frank Langella, 1979

Gary Oldman, 1992

WHEN NEWS OF PRINCESS DIANA'S
DEATH SPREAD AROUND THE GLOBE,
MANY PEOPLE—EVEN THOSE WHO
DIDN'T THINK THEY WERE ESPECIALLY
SMITTEN WITH THE WALESES—FOUND THEM-
SELVES SURPRISINGLY MOVED. IT IS ALWAYS
TRAGIC TO SEE A LIFE CUT SHORT. BUT SOME-
THING WAS VERY DIFFERENT HERE.

WHY WE LOVED HER

There have been women more beautiful, more naturally stylish.

But one of the things we loved about Diana was that she was not a ready-made stunner —though she did have the raw material. As a neophyte royal she made fashion faux pas and had her share of bad-hair days. Still, she could charm the camera and the public with an unpracticed upward glance of her blue eyes that quietly asked for approval. And so she received it—from her subjects, if not always from her prince. For years she appeared not even to know that she was beautiful, which made her all the more appealing. Diana brought glamour to the world without making it seem unattainable.

Others may have shown more devotion to charitable causes.

But we loved Diana for her compassion, particularly when she turned unrelenting press attention into an agent for good. Diana inspired changes in attitude—and the opening of checkbooks—with her fearless, hands-on approach. She embraced AIDS patients when others shied away. She walked through countries infested

TIM GRAHAM/SYGMA (1997)

with landmines. She talked about her own struggles with bulimia because she thought it would help other victims. Most of all, Diana displayed a bewitching weakness for

JULIAN PARKER/GAMMA LIAISON (1990)

children. But while her empathy for the young and for strangers in need was enormous, her deepest commitment was always apparent: Her two sons ruled her heart and remained her greatest loves.

OCTOBER
NOVEMBER
DECEMBER

Shattered Lives

Earthquakes in central Italy brought a ceiling of the 13th century Basilica of Saint Francis of Assisi crashing down, fragmenting priceless frescoes and killing four people. The death toll rose as aftershocks rumbled for more than a month. Here, a restorer pieces together a fresco of Saint Rufinus, protector of Assisi, as townspeople struggle to do the same with their lives.

ALBERTO PIZZOLI/SYGMA

110

Attorney General Janet Reno says she **does not have sufficient evidence** to appoint an independent counsel to investigate possible fund-raising abuses by the President during his 1995–1996 reelection campaign. Two days later the White House will release portions of videotapes, recorded by its own television crews, showing the President entertaining Democratic donors at 44 coffee meetings.

The largest and most complete *Tyrannosaurus rex* skeleton ever found is bought at auction for $8.4 million by Chicago's Field Museum (with funding from Disney and McDonald's). The **65-million-year-old fossil,** recovered in South Dakota in 1990, is nicknamed Sue after its discoverer, Susan Hendrickson.

Spice Rack

Paparazzi snapped away at the Spice Girls dolls' debut in London. The real-life Girls continued their reign in the spotlight long after many had anticipated their 15 minutes would be up. When Prince Charles and younger son Harry met the live Girls during a trip to South Africa, Charles proclaimed it "the second-best day of my life." He didn't say what the first was.

BEN CURTIS/PA NEWS

A rally in Washington, D.C., attracts several hundred thousand Promise Keepers. Members of **the expanding Christian men's movement,** they assemble to share their belief that a newfound commitment to God and family is the cure for many societal ills. Some feminists protest the group's emphasis on men as heads of household as a "danger to women's rights."

Elton John's "Candle in the Wind 1997" ships **more copies than any single in history.** John performed this version of the song, with revised lyrics by Bernie Taupin, at the funeral of Princess Diana.

Hurricane Pauline devastates the coast of Mexico, killing 230 people. In the poorest sections of Acapulco, 40 lives are lost (nearby luxury resorts and hotels are spared). Meteorologists in the area surmise that the storm may have been **influenced by El Niño,** a cyclical ocean current that is causing a gradual warming of the Pacific.

Together We Stand

Inspired by 1995's Million Man March, hundreds of thousands of African American women gathered in Philadelphia to demonstrate their commitment to one another and their communities. Marchers rejoiced as speakers stressed the importance of unity in battling woes from drug addiction to fractured families. Brenda Burgess, director of ceremonies, summed up: "See what we can do when we work together!"

115

HARF ZIMMERMANN/OSTKREUZ

OCT. 16 Revealed: Twins born in Georgia in August were the result of the U.S.'s first successful pregnancy using **eggs that had been frozen,** thawed and fertilized. This success for the 39-year-old mother, who had no eggs of her own because of premature menopause, may lead to benefits for many other infertile or older women.

OCT. 19 Hungarian-born American financier George Soros **pledges up to $500 million** to aid Russian health and education programs over the next three years. The billionaire, who has given $260 million to Russia since 1994, will be a bigger donor to the country this year than will the U.S. government.

OCT. 20 The Justice Department asks a federal court to hold **Microsoft in civil contempt** for violating a 1995 court order that prohibits it from monopolizing the Internet browser market. Attorney General Janet Reno will seek a fine of $1 million for each day that Microsoft is not in compliance with the original order.

Curves of Steel

People flocked to see American architect Frank Gehry's daring design for the new Guggenheim Museum in Bilbao, Spain, even before it was completed. Swirling walls of titanium contributed to the $100 million construction costs, but when the building was done, it was hailed as an act of bravery and vision. "It's a victory for all," wrote critic Herbert Muschamp.

OCT. 26 The Florida Marlins, in only their fifth season as a major-league team, become **World Series champions,** beating the Cleveland Indians in a seven-game battle. The series MVP is 22-year-old Florida pitcher Livan Hernandez, whose mother is permitted by Cuban officials to enter the U.S. to see her son's team win the final game.

OCT. 27 A worldwide **plunge in stock prices** erases more than 7 percent from the Dow Jones industrial average, forcing the New York Stock Exchange to halt trading. In points (554.26), the decline is the largest ever. The Dow had been at an all-time high and will rally the next day to close up 337.17 points.

OCT. 29 When Chinese President Jiang Zemin meets with President Clinton, the two men clash on **the issue of human rights:** Jiang defends his nation's actions in Tiananmen Square in 1989, and Clinton maintains that China's "continuing reluctance to tolerate political dissent" prevents the country from gaining global support.

Live by the Sword ...

It wasn't exactly a demonstration of democracy in action. A four-month civil war between past and current leaders ripped through the Congo Republic. In the end, the soldiers of former dictator Gen. Denis Sassou Nguesso prevailed. Taking over the Brazzaville palace of departed President Pascal Lissouba, they entered his private salon and took aim at this portrait, shouting, "We will kill you, assassin!"

119

NOV. 1 For the first time in the history of the four major professional sports leagues in America, **a female officiates** a regular-season game. Violet Palmer, 33, formerly the head of WNBA officials, referees an NBA matchup between the Dallas Mavericks and the Vancouver Grizzlies. Dee Kantner, 37, will also call NBA games.

NOV. 5 Joining George and Barbara Bush at the dedication ceremonies of the **George Bush Presidential Library** in College Station, Tex., are: President Clinton and the First Lady; Jimmy Carter and Gerald Ford and their wives, Rosalynn and Betty; Nancy Reagan; and Lady Bird Johnson. Former President Ronald Reagan, suffering from Alzheimer's disease, is unable to attend.

NOV. 5 The ancient practice of acupuncture is deemed, by a panel convened by the National Institutes of Health, **a safe and effective therapy** for some health conditions. The remedy could become standard treatment for such common problems as nausea caused by chemotherapy or pregnancy, discomfort from dental surgery and lower back pain.

Some Are Happy

Deep rifts opened between England and America, as well as between working and nonworking parents, when a jury found English au pair Louise Woodward guilty of the murder in Massachusetts of eight-month-old Matthew Eappen. The judge reduced the conviction to involuntary manslaughter and the sentence to time served. Supporters in an English pub cheered; the Eappens grieved.

PETER BYRNE

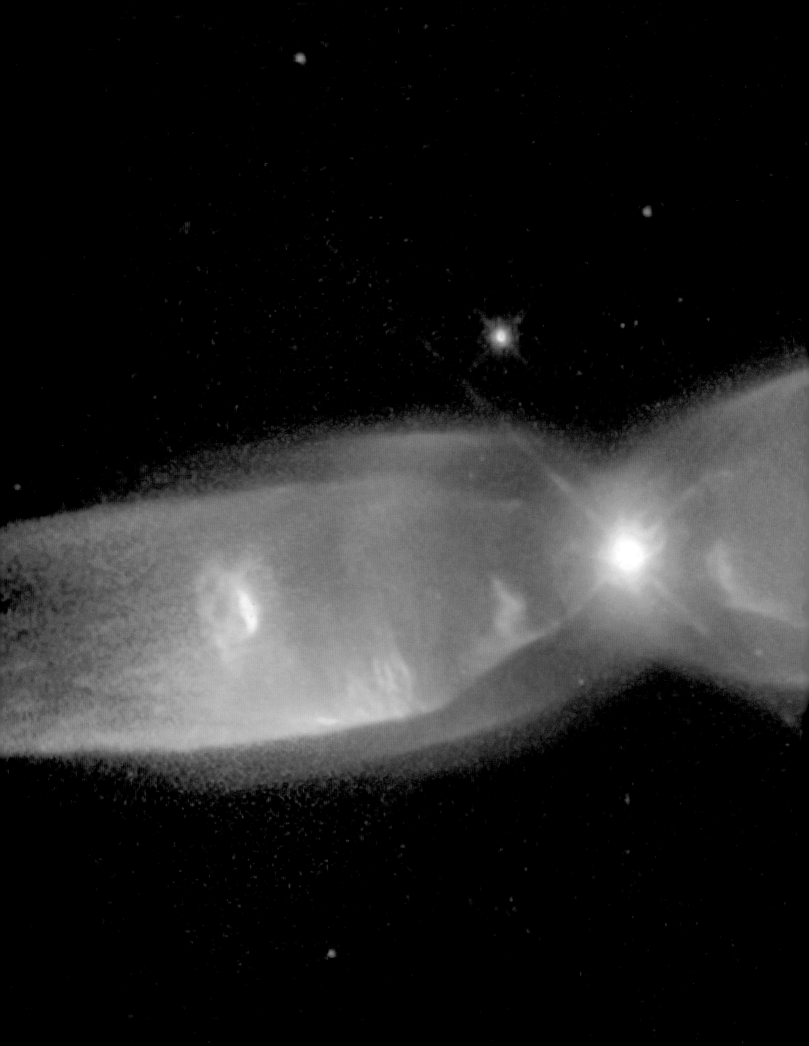

NOV. 5 Insurance companies for two doctors and a Chicago hospital agree to pay $10.6 million, the largest-ever settlement in a "memory therapy" case. The lawsuit alleged that psychotherapists brainwashed a woman, implanting **false memories** of joining a satanic cult and taking part in cannibalism.

NOV. 12 The FBI formally ends its investigation of the crash of TWA Flight 800, having "found **absolutely no evidence**" of a criminal act. The National Transportation Safety Board will continue to probe possible mechanical failure on the Boeing 747, which crashed on July 17, 1996, killing all 230 people on board. Any official speculation about a missile or bomb destroying the plane is laid to rest.

NOV. 16 China releases a leading dissident, Wei Jingsheng, allowing him to travel to Detroit for medical treatment. Wei, 47, jailed since 1979 for advocating democracy, suffers from hypertension. His release—a concession to international pressure—does not improve **China's climate for human rights.** Wei will remain in exile, unlikely ever to return to his native country.

Life Cycle

This is how certain stars die— and how others will be born. Thanks to the latest crop of dazzling images from the Hubble Space Telescope, scientists now believe that violent death throes (like these outbursts of dispersing gases) distribute heavier elements through space. In the spirit of recycling, they will join with emerging planets and stars.

123

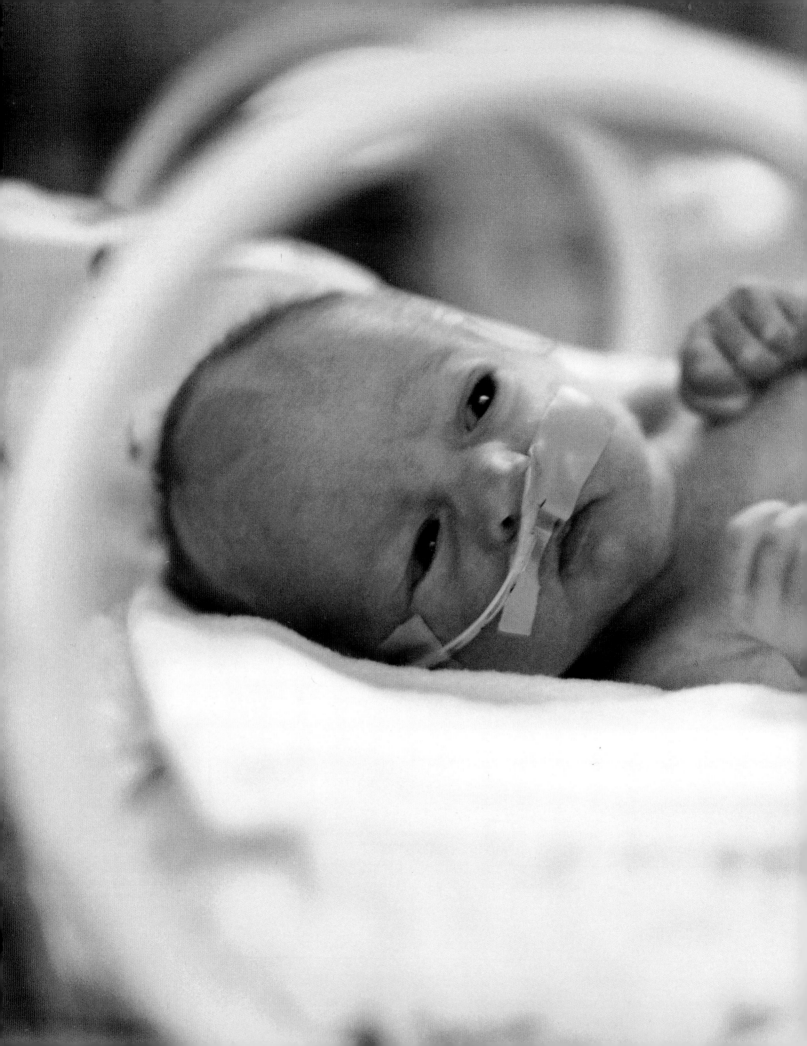

COURTESY OF IOWA METHODIST MEDICAL CENTER

NOV. 17 Teamsters president Ron Carey, whose reelection had been nullified in August pending an investigation, is barred from running again after a court-appointed monitor finds that he **used laundered union funds** to finance his campaign. The new favorite in the upcoming race is James P. Hoffa, son of the legendary Teamsters leader.

NOV. 21 U.N. arms inspectors are allowed into Iraq, ending a tense three-week standoff. President Saddam Hussein, apparently attempting to evade detection of his country's **weapons of mass destruction,** had expelled the inspectors, calling them spies.

DEC. 1 Fourteen-year-old Michael Carneal opens fire on an early-morning prayer circle at Heath High School in West Paducah, Ky., **killing three girls** and wounding five other students. The killer, who will later confess, is carrying five guns stolen from a neighbor's garage and uses a .22-caliber semiautomatic pistol. The incident comes only two months after two students were killed in a shooting at a Pearl, Miss., school; nevertheless, according to the National School Safety Center, the trend in the past few years is toward less violence in the nation's schools.

Seventh Heaven

When 29-year-old Iowan Bobbi McCaughey gave birth to seven babies in the span of six minutes, the biggest surprise was how healthy they were. Exhibit A: Kenneth Robert, dubbed Hercules, who supported his siblings in the womb. As donations for the world's only surviving septuplets poured in, those of us who've struggled to get just one infant to sleep sent our best wishes.

125

The judge presiding over the Dow Chemical Company **breast implant case** rules against a class-action lawsuit. Instead of including 1,800 claims of implants causing illness, the trial will cover only eight plaintiffs.

Despite pressure from FBI Director Louis J. Freeh and others, Attorney General Reno **refuses to seek** an independent prosecutor to investigate fund-raising telephone calls made by President Clinton and Vice President Gore. Republicans react angrily to the decision; however, Reno vows that the Justice Department's own inquiry on campaign finance will continue.

The body of M. Larry Lawrence, former U.S. ambassador to Switzerland, is exhumed from Arlington National Cemetery after it was proved that he had **fabricated a record** of heroic merchant marine service in World War II and therefore did not qualify for burial with honors.

Pieced Together

More than a year after TWA Flight 800 exploded, crash investigators had painstakingly reassembled the fragmented 747 to determine the cause of the disaster. The conclusion: no bomb, no terrorist. A mechanical malfunction—creating just one tiny but deadly spark—was most likely to blame for all that destruction.

JAN STALLER /NTSB

DEC. 23 Terry Nichols is convicted of conspiring to bomb the Oklahoma City federal building **but acquitted of murder.** The Denver jury differentiates the roles of Nichols and Timothy McVeigh, previously convicted on 11 counts of their joint indictment and sentenced to death. As the year ends, the penalty phase of Nichols's trial begins.

DEC. 24 The Clinton administration joins other nations in supplying South Korea, which is suffering a **severe economic crisis,** with an immediate $10 billion loan. The U.S. had already committed $5 billion to the International Monetary Fund's planned $57 billion bailout of South Korea, but that relief is to be disbursed gradually.

DEC. 31 To combat a rare outbreak of avian influenza in humans, Hong Kong destroys 1.4 million chickens and other feathered creatures. Because the **virus is transmitted to humans** by birds (four people have died and 10 others been infected), it is hoped that the slaughter will prevent an epidemic.

Closing Time?

George Foreman's year had a festive start: He and Muhammad Ali shared an onstage Oscar celebration for the 1996 documentary of their "Rumble in the Jungle." But near year's end, the seemingly eternal 48-year-old former champ (seen here after a November workout) announced his retirement. "I had a wonderful career," he said—just before he changed his mind and renounced his announcement.

GUESS WHAT'S INSIDE?

TOY SURPRISE

Blissèd State

He didn't need a comeback year; he never went away after all. But Buddha's been making the scene in 1997, with a boost from the likes of Brad Pitt and Martin Scorsese.

130

4TH

FOURTH QUARTERLY REPORT

Autumn? *Again?* The Marlins bade a euphoric farewell to summer; Halloween came and went; and Saddam Hussein again took to the blustering and posturing that had embroiled our country in war at the start of the decade. As that threat showed signs of subsiding, we turned in earnest to giving thanks: that some of the world's most horrific natural disasters did not strike our shores, that we could close out the year in peace, that all seven babies seemed to be O.K. And that there were no more shopping days until Christmas.

"The most difficult thing is to ignite a house or kill a man for the first time, but afterwards everything becomes routine."
—Former Croatian militiaman **Miro Bajramovic**, discussing the 86 people whose deaths he was responsible for

"Your parents did it. How cool can it be?"
—Message on a **Mississippi billboard,** part of a campaign to discourage young people from smoking

"He brought home the bacon, but I shopped for it, cooked it and cleaned up after it." —**Lorna Wendt,** on why she deserves her $20 million divorce settlement from GE executive Gary Wendt

"I blew it." —**George Bush,** in a new biography, on choosing Dan Quayle as his 1988 running mate

"Black women have taken care of everyone else since the time we've been in this country. We've taken care of white women, white men, white children ... our own men, our own children. And now it's time that we take care of ourselves."
—**Phile Chionesu,** the Philadelphia businesswoman and mother who conceived the Million Woman March

"I am a good person, and I've never had any situation like this come up before."
—**Latrell Sprewell** of the Golden State Warriors, after throttling his coach

"It is accurate to say that if we had it to do all over again, we would do it differently." —**Tom Koby,** Boulder, Colo., police chief, on the JonBenét Ramsey murder investigation

"**I am sure that the average movie fan could learn to distinguish between Ingrid Bergman and Harpo.**"

—**Groucho Marx,** in a letter to Warner Bros. (read aloud at a Library of Congress gala this fall) explaining why his 1946 film *A Night in Casablanca* would not infringe on the other *Casablanca*

"Anything that
says 'healthy'
I stay away from....
Giving up butter, for instance,
means that in about
two years you will be covered
in dandruff."

—85-year-old chef **Julia Child,** dismissing the trend toward fat-free foods

"My wife thinks I'm at
Promise Keepers."

—Slogan on T-shirts worn by three fans at an Orioles-Mariners play-off game

Sweet Sue?

As you can see from the teeth, this *T. Rex* (Tyrant Lizard King), now at Chicago's Field Museum, was pure ferocity—all 40 feet of her.

$33,000,000 Reported value of Michael Jordan's current one-year contract with the NBA's Chicago Bulls

$50,000 Highest salary paid to any player in the WNBA

Happy Birthday!

To celebrate 100 years of slurping and jiggling, both Campbell's and Jell-O introduced new flavors this year, cream of mushroom with roasted garlic, and sparkling white grape, respectively.

They Made Us Proud

Jody Williams

After the American director of the International Campaign to Ban Land Mines was awarded the Nobel Peace Prize, she encouraged President Clinton to add the U.S.'s signature to a treaty abolishing the hidden killers.

CHRISTMAS

Sano di Pietro 1997 National Gallery of Art

USA 32

American holly 32 USA

Season's Greetings

Resolved to be pancultural *and* festive as the holidays neared, the Post Office drew from both the National Gallery and the local nursery.

Forever Young
Radio City Music Hall celebrated its 65th anniversary in 1997, but the Rockettes remain ageless.

"I'd find it difficult to ride on the back of something like that myself, but Reg is showbiz."
—Rolling Stone **Keith Richards,** after Elton John (Reginald Dwight) sang at Princess Diana's funeral

Stamps took wing with a series commemorating American fighter planes.

Rookie of the Year
Buddy

Empty-nest syndrome can strike anywhere. The universal solution? Get a pet. So, with apologies to Socks, Bill Clinton brought this youngster into the White House. The chocolate Labrador puppy clearly had that take-me-home look in his eyes.

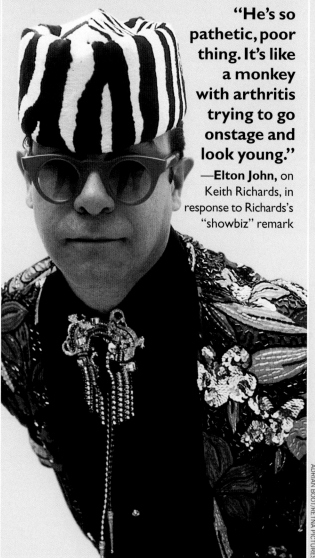

"He's so pathetic, poor thing. It's like a monkey with arthritis trying to go onstage and look young."
—**Elton John,** on Keith Richards, in response to Richards's "showbiz" remark

It Just Got Harder to Be Green

Thanksgiving Day brought strong winds to the Macy's parade in New York. Kermit the Frog and the Cat in the Hat were among the victims of these deflationary times.

ALL THE PRESIDENTS' TAPES

Transcripts of privately recorded conversations from the Kennedy, Johnson and Nixon administrations—all published in 1997 books—offer a revealing glimpse into the pressures of our nation's highest office. For some of us, these words triggered chilling memories; for others, they were a harsh reality-based lesson in civics.

JOHN F. KENNEDY

President Kennedy met with his advisers to discuss the U.S. military's discovery of Soviet nuclear arms in Cuba. After these deliberations, he would impose a U.S. naval blockade around Cuba.

Oct. 18, 1962—The U.S. considers whether to warn Soviet leader Nikita Khrushchev before attacking the Cuban missile sites.

Undersecretary of State George Ball: [If] we strike without warning, that's like Pearl Harbor. It's the kind of conduct that one might expect of the Soviet Union.... And I have a feeling that this 24 hours to Khrushchev is really indispensable.

JFK: And then if he says: "If you are going to do that, we're going to grab Berlin.".... He'll grab Berlin, of course. Then either way it would be we lost Berlin, because of these missiles...

Secretary of Defense Robert S. McNamara: Well, when we're talking about taking Berlin, what do we mean exactly? That they take it with Soviet troops?

JFK?: That's what I would think....

Unidentified: ... then what do we do?

Ball: Go to general war.

JFK: You mean a nuclear exchange?

Unidentified: Mmm-hmm.

Unidentified: That's right.

The Kennedy Tapes: Inside the White House During the Cuban Missile Crisis, edited by Ernest R. May and Philip D. Zelikow, Harvard University Press

Taking Charge: The Johnson White House Tapes, 1963-1964, edited by Michael R. Beschloss, Simon & Schuster

Abuse of Power: The New Nixon Tapes, edited by Stanley I. Kutler, The Free Press

LYNDON B. JOHNSON

The instant he was sworn into office—aboard Air Force One, hours after the November 1963 assassination of JFK—President Johnson was faced with defining America's role in Vietnam. By mid-1964 he was tortured by the issue.

May 27, 1964—Should the U.S. be in or out of Vietnam? Johnson discussed his war worries with his national security adviser, McGeorge Bundy:

LBJ: I stayed awake last night thinking of this thing . . . it looks to me like we're getting into another Korea. . . . I don't think that we can fight them ten thousand miles away from home. . . . I don't think it's worth fighting for and I don't think that we can get out. It's just the biggest damned mess that I ever saw.

Bundy: It's an awful mess.

LBJ: . . . I was looking at this sergeant of mine [Kenneth Gaddis, LBJ's valet] this morning. Got six little old kids . . . and I just thought about ordering his kids in there and what in the hell am I ordering him out there for? . . . What the hell is Vietnam worth to me? . . . What is it worth to this country?

RICHARD M. NIXON

That President Nixon taped his private conversations is commonly known. But, while Kennedy and Johnson selectively recorded themselves, Nixon's taping device was voice-activated. At times he seemed to forget that the tape was running.

May 10, 1973—The President meets with his former chief of staff, H.R. Haldeman:

Nixon: Bob, I don't think people give a [expletive] about the CIA thing. I don't really think they care. I don't think they care about bugging Ellsberg [the former National Security Council aide who leaked the Pentagon Papers—a secret history of the Vietnam war—to *The New York Times* in 1971]. . . . I know that they care much about bugging the Goddamn Pentagon—I mean, the—

Haldeman: Watergate.

Nixon: Watergate. I think the cover-up deal was a problem and the obstruction of justice was a problem in the sense that it looks like we've tried to—what I mean—we were not carrying out *the law*, so-called.

Haldeman: Yeah.

Nixon: That is a problem. . . . But the main thing is that all this crap about the President should resign. . . .

Haldeman: Don't even listen.

Nixon: Nobody should even ever raise such things. . . . [If] I walk out of this office, you know, on this [expletive] stuff, why it would leave a mark on the American political system. It's unbelievable.

135

LATE GREATS

MOTHER TERESA

WHEN THEY TALK of saints, they ask, "Where's the miracle?" The miracle was that a tiny woman in the fetid slums of Calcutta resolved to spend her life serving the poorest of the poor—thereby growing to be immense. "Near the end she was very old, wrinkled, tired, sick—and beautiful," says Father Gerald O'Collins of Rome's Pontifical Gregorian University. "There's a strange beauty about holy old people." Father O'Collins can't be sure if Mother Teresa, who died at 87, was a saint but says: "She's certainly with Jesus. You could tell as she died. She was ready."

RAGHU RAI/MAGNUM PHOTOS (1983)

GIANNI VERSACE

HIS OVER-THE-TOP trademark look—loud colors, flashy prints, depth-defying necklines and thigh-high hemlines—attracted fashion extroverts by the shopping bagful and built a billion-dollar business. He was one of the first designers to turn fashion shows into runway rock operas. He hobnobbed with blue bloods and celebs from Princess Diana to Madonna. But for all his outward excesses, this family-loving 50-year-old son of an Italian dressmaker was surprisingly down-to-earth. Returning from his daily solo walk, he was gunned down by serial killer Andrew Cunanan in front of his Miami Beach home.

JACQUES COUSTEAU

HE HAD SET HIS SIGHTS ON BECOMING a pilot for the French navy before a car accident derailed his plans. Swimming daily to regain strength in his injured arms, he dreamed of a watery freedom, released from the need to surface to breathe. From those dreams came the scuba system, which opened up vast areas of ocean to wondrous exploration. By the time he died, at 87, Jacques-Yves Cousteau was a legendary explorer and filmmaker; more, he was the familiar, friendly symbol of earth's oceans and of the movement to protect them for future generations.

CECIL BEATON (1940)

PAMELA
HARRIMAN

HER NAME—Pamela Digby Churchill Hayward

Harriman—suggests a life lived in the company of many

men and in proximity to power. She was the daughter of a

baron, the daughter-in-law and confidante of a British

prime minister, the wife of a Broadway producer and,

later, of a former New York governor. Not to mention

lover to a prince and a Rothschild. But she was more than

the sum of her romantic résumé. ("The amount of people

that I read about that I've slept with . . . it's extraordinary!")

With the money and access that her birthright and

connections brought, Harriman at last made a name for

herself: Her PamPAC channeled funds to the Democratic

party during the Reagan and Bush years. Her support

helped land Clinton in the White House and Harriman in

the office of the U.S. ambassador to France. There the

consummate diplomat worked until her death at age 76.

TED ALLEN/MPTV (1936)

IT COULDN'T HAVE HAPPENED TO A NICER GUY: early success, true love, respect from his peers and the adoration of his fans. Hard to hold it against him, for the star of *Mr. Smith Goes to Washington*, *The Philadelphia Story* and *It's a Wonderful Life* brought an unironic joy to generations. The child of a Pennsylvania hardware store owner, James Maitland Stewart first took to the stage as an accordionist. Later he would slide his long, gangly legs and his everyman persona into some 80 films; the nice-guy-made-good, who died at 89, was among the most gifted practitioners of his craft.

JIMMY STEWART

BETTY SHABAZZ

CHESTER HIGGINS (1972)

LEFT TO RAISE SIX young daughters alone after witnessing the 1965 assassination of her husband, Malcolm X, Betty Shabazz had every reason to come apart at the seams. But she held it all together—herself, her

family and her husband's legacy—with strength and dignity, earning a doctorate along the way. That resilience was not enough, however, to overcome the terrible burns she suffered at the hands of her troubled grandson Malcolm, 12, who torched her apartment in apparent anger at having been sent to live with her. Shabazz endured five operations before succumbing to her injuries at the age of 61.

ARNOLD NEWMAN (1959)

WILLEM DE KOONING

HE WAS, IN HIS WAY, a most traditional artist. But de Kooning, 92, fearlessly redefined traditions even as he cherished them. Unlike his fellow abstract expressionists in the 1950s, the brash young painter clung to the human form, most passionately the female figure, as the essential vehicle for both aesthetic observation and intense self-revelation. Later the more mature artist created airy abstractions that he had scraped down and repainted until they were worked into a state of seemingly effortless lightness. At all times, his work put us in intimate contact with a distinctly human mix of sensory delight and emotional turmoil.

ALLEN GINSBERG

THE BEST OF HIS poems were of madness: *Kaddish* was a tribute to his insane mother; *Howl* to the best mad minds of his generation. He was a little mad himself, but it was a merry madness (he was kicked out of Cuba for saying Che Guevara was "cute") that lasted for 70 years, until silenced by cancer in April. "I am flesh and blood," Ginsberg wrote half a century ago, "but my mind is the focus of much lightning." May his thunder never cease.

MILLIE

SHE SHARED A BED WITH THE
President, became a single mother while
living in the White House, then penned
a best-selling memoir that won raves
from one unlikely *New York Times* book
reviewer. Who was the literary critic?
Garfield, the comic-strip cat. The author?
Mildred Kerr Bush, the real-life dog. The

opus? *Millie's Book: As Dictated to Barbara
Bush,* which raised nearly $900,000
for literacy programs and lifted the spirits
of many fans in and out of D.C. The
floppy-eared English springer spaniel
died at age 11—that's 71 in human
years—in Kennebunkport, Maine.

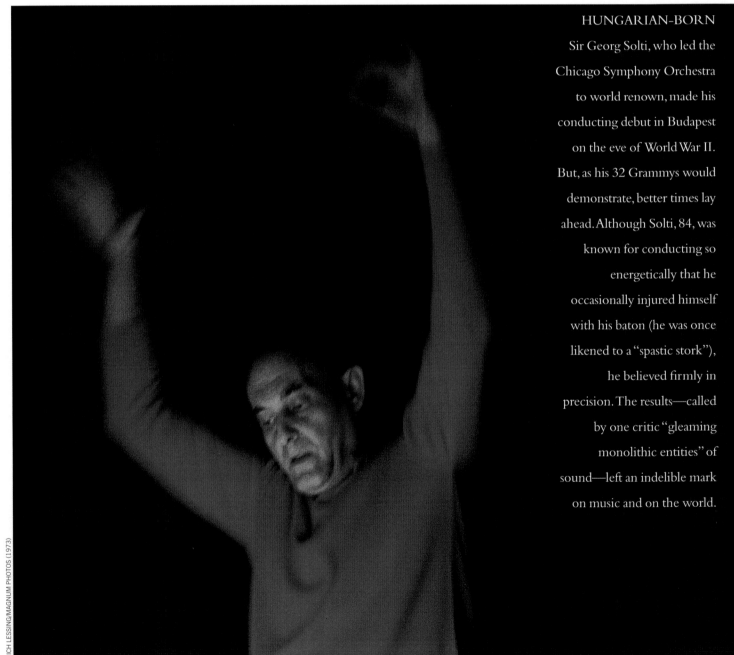

GEORG
SOLTI

HUNGARIAN-BORN
Sir Georg Solti, who led the
Chicago Symphony Orchestra
to world renown, made his
conducting debut in Budapest
on the eve of World War II.
But, as his 32 Grammys would
demonstrate, better times lay
ahead. Although Solti, 84, was
known for conducting so
energetically that he
occasionally injured himself
with his baton (he was once
likened to a "spastic stork"),
he believed firmly in
precision. The results—called
by one critic "gleaming
monolithic entities" of
sound—left an indelible mark
on music and on the world.

NOTORIOUS B.I.G.

THE RAP ARTIST BORN
Christopher Wallace died as he lived—
in a cloud of controversy. Murdered
last March at age 24 in an unsolved
drive-by shooting, the former drug
hustler "dropped science" about life on
the streets and in the limelight that
rang true to listeners—and rang up
sales in the millions. Neither his
frequent run-ins with the law nor the
mislabeling of his music as gangsta
rap could detract from his talent.

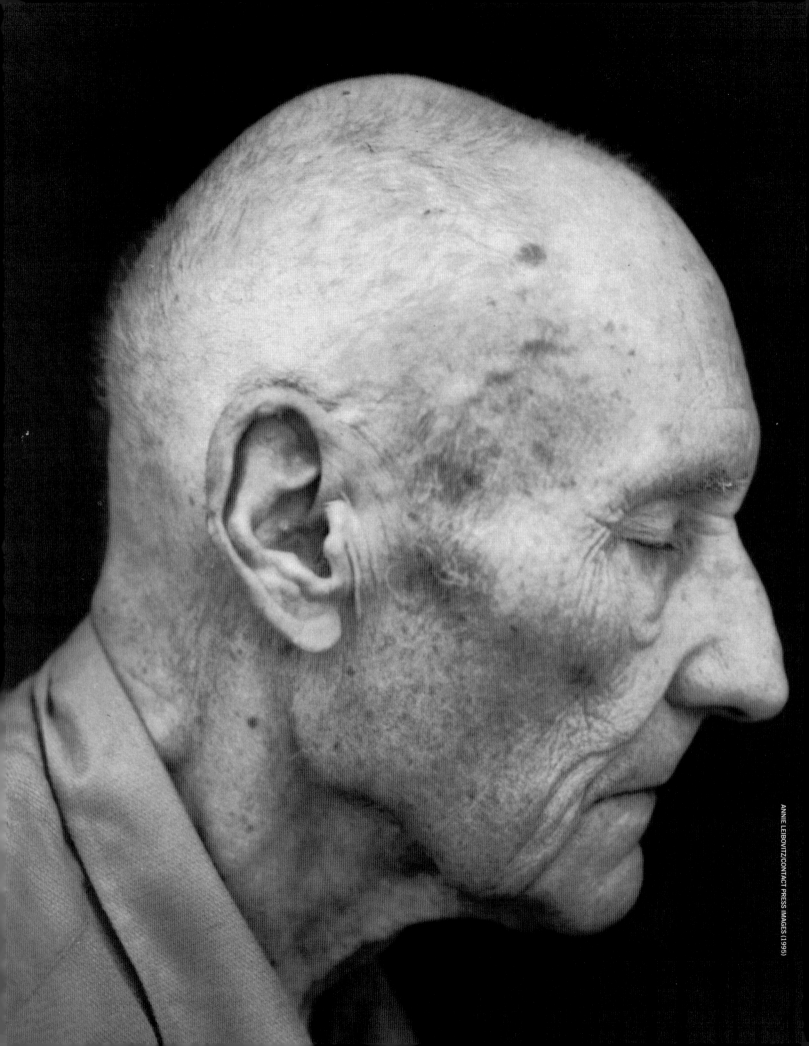

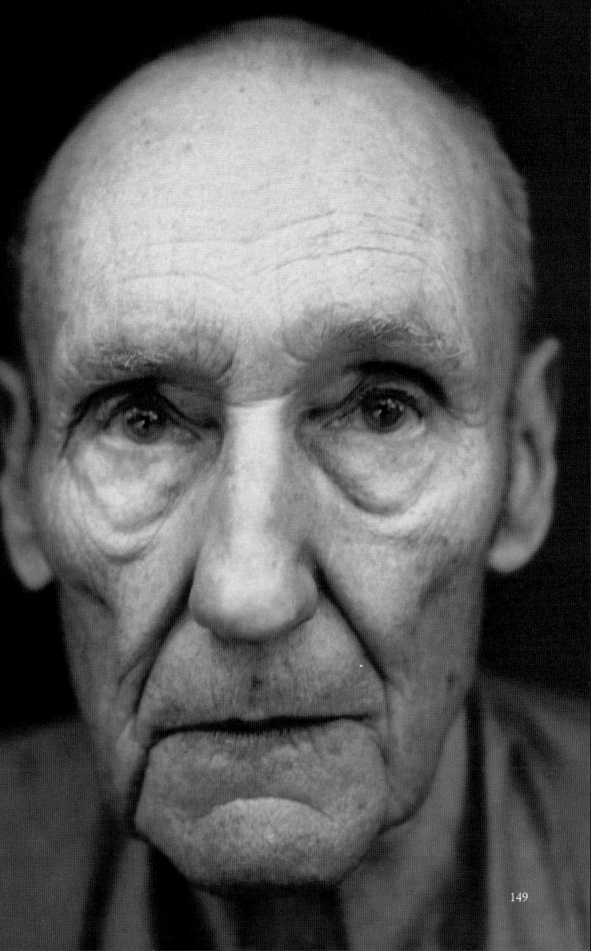

WILLIAM S. BURROUGHS

HE WAS THE BELOVED patriarch of them all: the Beats, the hippies, even the punk rockers. When he died at 83, he had just made a video with U2. It's a miracle that avant-garde novelist William S. Burroughs lived past 30. A brilliant St. Louis blue blood, he spent 15 years as a heroin addict, drifting from Greenwich Village to Tangier. En route he sampled a wide variety of sex and drugs and became the mentor of two young writers named Ginsberg and Kerouac. His 1959 classic, *Naked Lunch*, was a junkie's free-form hallucination. Denounced as obscene blather, acclaimed as a work of twisted genius, it earned Burroughs a permanent place in the pantheon of hip.

149

ROY LICHTENSTEIN

LIFE ONCE ASKED, "IS HE THE WORST ARTIST IN THE U.S.?"
Perhaps we were affronted by art that portrayed the flotsam of a culture—bubble
gum wrappers and comic books. But Roy Lichtenstein and his fellow pop artists
understood people's fascination with those simple artifacts. His later paintings
were more likely to allude to Matisse or Miró. When he died at 73, he had earned
the reverent affection befitting a graceful, whimsical modern master.

CHARLES KURALT

AFTER COVERING THE VIETNAM WAR, he grew tired of grimness. So in 1967, Charles Kuralt set off in a secondhand camper, searching for the "resolutely insignificant" along his nation's byways. What he found, in ordinary people and places, was extraordinary beauty—and for 13 years he shared it on TV in a series of reports called *On the Road*. Kuralt eloquently celebrated American originals: lumberjacks, beer can collectors, a nonagenarian carver of carousel horses. He was 62 when his big heart failed on July 4—"an inappropriate death," said his old boss, former CBS chief Howard Stringer, "on a most appropriate day."

BEN HOGAN

BY DYING AT 84 IN THE season of Tiger Woods's ascension, the great Hogan—winner of 63 tournaments, including nine majors, and as dominant a player as has ever walked the fairways—was inevitably recalled as the Tiger of an earlier era. But where is the intersection of Hogan and Woods? As muscular and short (5'8") as Tiger is lithe and lean, as taciturn as Tiger is gregarious, the former caddie from Fort Worth seemed to share nothing with the prodigy from Southern California. Ah, but look at the eyes. "They had a piercing quality," Jim Murray wrote of Hogan years ago and could write of Woods tomorrow. "They were the eyes of a circling bird of prey; fearless, fierce; the pupils no more than dots in their imperious centers. They weren't the eyes of a loser."

RED SKELTON

HE SPENT SO MUCH TIME TAKING PRATFALLS for laughs that his knees were finished by age 40. Shrugging off the discomfort, he rose to national prominence in radio and moved to television for a remarkable run on CBS, from 1953 to 1970. Always keeping his material clean and his audiences in stitches, Richard Bernard Skelton created indelible characters like Clem Kadiddlehopper and the Mean Widdle Kid. He toured college campuses after his show's cancellation (never really losing a measure of bitterness toward CBS) and, in his spare time, liked to paint pictures of clowns. His customary farewell serves as a fitting epitaph for a top clown: "Good night, and God bless."

ROBERT MITCHUM

HIS CLASSIC CHARACTERS—THE doomed detective in *Out of the Past,* the murderous preacher in *The Night of the Hunter,* the sadistic stalker in *Cape Fear*—were cynical outsiders given to languid wit and sudden violence. Those hooded eyes looked as if they'd seen it all, and they had. Before drifting to Hollywood in 1943, Mitchum boxed, brawled, hitched freights, toiled as a deckhand, served time on a chain gang. He made light of the acting trade—"It sure beats working"—but Mitchum, who died at 79, was a disciplined craftsman. Playing the hero or the fiend, he was one of the screen's great avatars of scary cool.

HE WAS THE ULTIMATE survivor: Deng Xiaoping endured the Long March of 1934; the bloodshed of World War II; famine; not one but three purges over six decades. At last, in 1978, he established himself as China's premier. It was Deng who freed his nation from the stranglehold of Maoist dogma yet held to Mao's belief that political power grows

DENG XIAOPING

out of the barrel of a gun—a gun he didn't hesitate to use in Tiananmen Square. Earth's most populous nation will forever remember Deng, 92, as both an economic liberator and a political tyrant.

JOHN
DENVER

AFTER FOLK-POP ICON JOHN
Denver's homemade two-seater plane crashed
into Monterey Bay, a witness described the
sound as "a hundred tons of concrete dropped
from the heavens." For his fans, Denver's
death at 53 hit with similar force. The singer
born Henry John Deutschendorf Jr. in
Roswell, N.Mex., celebrated love and the
outdoors with homespun simplicity. His 1971
hit "Take Me Home, Country Roads"
secured his status with fans, if not with critics,
who routinely mocked his syrupy tunes as so
much Muzak. His response? "I want people
to feel the goodness in their own lives."

CHRIS CUFFARO/OUTLINE (1996)

NINA LEEN (1949)

LARRY BURROWS (1960)

CHRIS FARLEY

LIKE HIS IDOL, JOHN BELUSHI, comic Chris Farley got his start as the funny fat guy in Chicago's Second City comedy troupe, then joined *Saturday Night Live* and starred in several movies. Offscreen as well, Farley was all too much like Belushi: His compulsive eating and alcohol and drug use led to his death at 33.

JAMES MICHENER

A FOUNDLING RAISED BY QUAKERS in Pennsylvania, Michener achieved fame and fortune with his 1947 debut, *Tales of the South Pacific,* and the Broadway and movie hits it spawned. When he died at 90, his many novels, including *Hawaii* and *Texas,* which crawled from geologic past to geopolitical present, had sold 100 million copies.

MOBUTU SESE SEKO

RECRUITED BY U.S. INTELLIGENCE services in the 1960s as an ally against communist expansion, the former journalist seized the reins of Africa's third-largest country in 1965. He changed its name from Congo to Zaire, amassed a fortune of perhaps $5 billion as his nation grew poorer—then died at 66, four months after fleeing a coup.

LYNN JOHNSON/AURORA (1987)

BRIAN QUIGLEY/OUTLINE (1993)

DAVID GAHR (1969)

WILLIAM BRENNAN

HE SAW HIMSELF AS A COMMON man; when appointed to the Supreme Court in 1956, Brennan said he felt like "a mule at the Kentucky Derby." But his sharp mind and elfin grin won over his thoroughbred colleagues. His liberal voice had an unequaled impact on American life, and when he died, at 91, even his adversaries hailed him.

MICHAEL KENNEDY

LIKE HIS SLAIN FATHER, ROBERT, he toiled for social causes. But accusations of sexual misconduct split his family apart and led his cousin John F. Kennedy Jr. to write: "[He] fell in love with youth and surrendered his judgment in the process." On New Year's Eve, playing ski-football on a mountain, Michael, 39, crashed into a tree and was killed.

LAURA NYRO

A PIONEER OF THE FREE-SPIRITED folk music that grew out of the early 1960s, she drew from soul, gospel and even Broadway to create a highly introspective sound. Her performances were intoxicating, but in the end she preferred to let artists like the Fifth Dimension popularize her compositions. Few knew Nyro had cancer before she died at 49.